HARRIET HARGRAVE

FROM
FIBER
TO
FABRIC

THE ESSENTIAL GUIDE TO
QUILTMAKING TEXTILES

C&T PUBLISHING

©1997 Harriet Hargrave

Editor: Lee M. Jonsson
Technical Editor: Diana Roberts
Copy Editor: Judith M. Moretz
Illustrations: Gretchen Schwarzenbach, GNS Graphics, and John M. Cram
Cover design: John M. Cram and Kathy Lee
Book design: John M. Cram and Diane Pedersen
Photography: Sharon Risedorph Photography, San Francisco, California; Cevin Brent Smith Photography, Raleigh, North Carolina; and Jim Egan Photography, Providence, Rhode Island
Interior mill shots: Cotton Incorporated, Raleigh, North Carolina, Cranston Print Works Company, Webster, Massachusetts, and Pendleton Woolen Mills, Portland, Oregon
Author photo: James Koch

Photographs in Chapter 8, 9, 13, and all chapter openers by Sharon Risedorph. Photographs in Chapters 3 and 6 by Cevin Brent Smith unless otherwise noted. Photographs in Chapters 4 and 7 by Jim Egan unless otherwise noted. Photographs in Chapter 5 by Pendleton Woolen Mills. Photographs in Chapter 12 by Harriet Hargrave.

Library of Congress Cataloging-in-Publication Data
Hargrave, Harriet.
    From fiber to fabric : the essential guide to quiltmaking textiles / Harriet Hargrave.
    p.   cm.
    Includes bibliographical references and index.
    ISBN 1-57120-025-8
    1. Cotton fabrics. 2. Quilts. 3. Patchwork--Equipment and supplies. I. Title.
TS1582.H37 1997
677'.21--dc21   96-45223
                                                CIP

Published by C&T Publishing
P.O. Box 1456
Lafayette, CA 94549

Printed in China

10 9 8 7 6 5 4 3 2 1

TABLE OF CONTENTS

ACKNOWLEDGMENTS

I want to sincerely thank Dr. Brent Smith, professor at North Carolina State University School of Textiles. His many hours of editing and correcting have given me the opportunity to pass on the most current information to you. I was indeed most fortunate when Nella Smith, his wife, attended one of my lectures in North Carolina, and got me in touch with her husband. Many, many thanks for your patience and time in helping with this project!

Many thanks also to Douglas Bryant, Janett Rice, Robert Beaulieu, Jane A. Barndt, and Jennifer Sampou Hensley, for their expertise and input which make this book a knowledgeable and up-to-date piece. My thanks also to Susan Neill, VIP Fabrics; Vicky Irvine, Cotton Incorporated; Kay Gibson, Pendleton Woolen Mills; Chris Marcinczyk, Cranston Printworks; Sharon Risedorph, Cevin Brent Smith, Jim Egan, and Jinny Beyer, for graciously providing photographs for the book.

My thanks to H. D. Wilbanks of Hobbs Bonded Fibers, who has spent hours with me over the years discussing batting and manufacturing processes as we have developed battings together. Untold hours of discussion, questions, and probing went into understanding the non-woven industry as it applies to quilters. His input has been invaluable. Another huge thanks goes to Danny Natividad, the chemical engineer for Hobbs Bonded Fibers. Many technical questions would have been left unanswered if it were not for his time and patience. Having the opportunity to discuss the batting desires of quilters with the brains behind the formulas was a true thrill for me. Cary Hobbs is also to be commended for allowing me to come into the factory with my camera and have full access to the employees. Seldom is one afforded the opportunity to move about so freely in a factory setting.

A big thanks also to Diana Roberts, John Cram, Kathy Lee, and Diane Pedersen who all helped with the book.

I don't know that this project would have ever been totally pulled together without the help of Lee Jonsson, my editor at C&T Publishing. She spent hours on the phone rounding up images for the fabric manufacturing process and on various other duties. A very special thank you goes to her for her patience with me and my schedule.

INTRODUCTION

While a tremendous amount of information has been published about the history of quiltmaking and the process of creating quilts, there has been a relative lack of information available to quilters about the medium with which we work—textiles. This lack of information has caused problems in the way we handle today's textiles and how they in turn perform. Because we invest so much of our time and money into our fabric, it is important we take responsibility for our textile education so that when we run into problems, we have the knowledge to find a solution.

This book was written to give you practical information about the fabrics, battings, and threads you use in your work. With a better understanding of how these textiles are made, what to consider when buying them, and how to care for them once you have bought them, you will have much more enjoyment and less stress as you create your wonderful quilts. After all, quiltmaking should be relaxing and therapeutic. It is my desire to create enough interest for you that you will continue reading and learning about the process, and have successful results with all your future projects.

COTTON IN QUILTMAKING

Cotton has historically been the fabric of choice for quilts. Fabrics made from cotton in the early quilts of the nineteenth century were called "wash goods." These fabrics could withstand the excessive washings needed because of daily use. They were generally known as calicoes, ginghams, chintzes, dimities, and challis.

Of these fabrics, calico remained the most widely used fabric in quiltmaking. Calicoes were generally printed with small-scale conventional patterns in one or two colors. They were sold as dress goods. The patterns were unending, and many of the patterns were printed for over fifty years. Because of their comfort, washability, and durability, cotton calicoes are still looked upon as the fabric of choice for today's quiltmakers.

However, when quilting began its revival in the 1970s, very little 100% cotton woven fabric was available. Woven cotton solids were unheard of, and the few prints made were of bright primary colors in tiny to small patterns. With this lack of cotton fabric, many quilters worked with fabrics made from cotton and polyester blends. These fabrics were readily available and were priced lower than the cottons. They also came in a wide variety of colors and prints. Many quilters liked the blends because they were strong, stable, colorfast, wrinkle resistant, and did not need ironing if prewashed.

After a few years of working with these blends, quilters began to realize there were some inherent problems with the polyester content in these fabrics. Polyester would not press flat because of the permanent press finish. It had a tendency to lift. The fabrics also tended to be more transparent than cottons, causing the seam allowances to shadow through the top layer of the quilt. Polyester is a stronger fiber than cotton; therefore, producers could reduce yarn thickness or the number of yarns per unit measurement and this would result in relative sheerness. *Pilling* is another problem quilters encountered when they washed the blend quilts a few times. (Pilling is the formation of groups of short or broken fibers on the surface of a fabric which are tangled together in the shape of a tiny ball called a pill. Synthetics and blends tend to pill when abrasion and friction are applied to their surfaces, whereas 100% cottons do not.) **Bearding** is another problem that occurs when polyester batting and synthetic fabrics are sandwiched together. The batting fibers migrate through the quilt top or backing and appear on the surface as white "fur" or "pills."

Cotton, on the other hand, feels good, is very absorbent, wears well, and softens with age. Because of the drawbacks with blends, and the continuing interest in quiltmaking, manufacturers took notice and began producing more and more cottons. The more they produced, the more we consumed, so that today we have a tremendous variety of colors, prints, and styles of cottons including gold embossed prints, woven plaids and stripes as well as numerous printed ones, authentic antique reproduction prints, and very contemporary, bold, bright exotic prints. It seems all we need to do is ask for a style of fabric and it is delivered. Thanks to many well-known quilters who work with the manufacturers' designers stylizing fabrics for us from a quilter's point of view, we truly do not want for cottons for our quilts any longer. This brings me to the reason I feel this is a most important book.

After all my years of teaching quiltmaking, I am still dismayed by what students are instructed to do with their fabrics and what they are not informed about with respect to the care of these wonderful fabrics. Many quilters feel that today's fabrics are not as good as they were one hundred years ago and that we must put them through a torture test to ensure they will not cause us problems after the quilts are done. I would like to propose a different approach—that we learn about the fabric first, both the qualities and drawbacks, and then learn how to work with the fabrics so we do not run into problems later.

Quiltmakers must become informed, conscientious consumers. Today many manufacturers are producing beautiful, top-quality fabrics for quiltmakers, and considering the price they are offered, we are extremely fortunate to have them available. The industry does, however, make different grades of fabrics for various end uses, and if we do not know about the different qualities and how to tell them apart, we are likely to purchase products that are not appropriate for quiltmaking. It doesn't make sense to work with inferior products and then criticize the entire industry for giving us a poor product. Once we know and understand what quality of fabric we need for our quilts, our expectations for the fabric we use can be met. As more conscientious consumers, we can begin to identify between high and inferior quality and choose to stay away from fabrics that do not perform to our specific needs. Knowing what the market demands, designers, manufacturers, converters, and retailers will continue producing top-quality fabric for our specific needs.

CHAPTER 1

CONSUMER EXPECTATIONS

STANDARDS AND EXPECTATIONS OF TODAY'S COTTONS

The Price of Cotton Fabric

Home sewers and quiltmakers have always been very price sensitive about fabric. There seems to be a link between the price of fabric and how much we will purchase. When I opened my quilt shop in 1980, the retail price of quilting fabric was $3.98/yard. At that time there was constant complaining about fabric being so expensive, and we felt we could not pay more. Sixteen years later, the average price is $6.70/yard, and we are still complaining about the price. While the price has increased with the normal rate of inflation, the quality of fabric has improved despite increasing labor costs, raw goods costs, manufacturing expenses, and governmental regulations due to environmental pressures. At the time of this writing, raw goods cost about 85¢/yard. That only leaves about $2.50/yard to get the finished goods to the retailer.

...while there is a need for each grade of fabric available, not all fabrics are necessarily appropriate for all end uses.

Evaluating the Quality of Cotton

Quilters need to be aware of which companies produce excellent fabrics at a price we accept, and which companies produce inferior goods at the same price; . . . which companies produce high-quality fabrics intended to last, and which companies produce second-quality goods that are not as durable or of as high a quality, but look the same. We need to consider not only the look of the fabric and its price, but also the quality of the fabric, the color and print, and its intended use. We cannot buy poor-quality fabric and then criticize the industry for what we agree to buy. We need to support and praise those companies that are working in our best interest.

Manufacturers and converters are not out to get us. They want our business. They are simply making fabrics to fill a consumer need at a specific price point. We send strong messages to these companies about what we want and do not want by what we purchase. In this way we really can make a difference in what becomes available to us.

As I mentioned, quilters need to evaluate quality in terms of the project's intended use. For example, if I am making a summer sundress for a five-year-old that will be worn only one season, I will probably shop for lower-quality fabric and look for the best price. I am not concerned with long-term durability. But if I am making a quilt for that same child, and I want her to enjoy it for many years, I need to take the quality of fabrics into consideration. Now I need durability, longevity of color and print; I need a high-quality fabric. Therefore, while there is a need for each grade of fabric available, not all fabrics are necessarily appropriate for all end uses.

Many quilters have avoided using fabrics that are more costly, even though they are better woven, better designed, and use higher-quality dyes and finishes. This viewpoint is short-sighted and self-depreciative. Quilters need to consider the value of their time.

The Value of Time

We no longer make quilts because we have to; we make them for our pleasure and relaxation as well as for creative, artistic, professional, and economic reasons. Therefore, we should treat ourselves to materials worthy of our skill and time. Consider that it takes the same one hundred hours to make a quilt from poor-quality fabrics as it does from high-quality fabrics. In the end, poor-quality materials will lead to a shortened life for the quilt. What is this saying about the value of your time? If we don't support the companies that provide us with top-quality goods for quiltmaking, and the price of fabric is the only factor we consider, we could very well see the fabric quality decrease each year in order to keep the price the same. You get what you pay for and you may only save $20.00 in materials by buying inferior-quality goods for a quilt.

Consider that it takes the same one hundred hours to make a quilt from poor-quality fabrics as it does from high-quality fabrics.

A Word About Fabric Manufacturing Standards

Today's fabrics are manufactured under standards and specifications principally for the apparel industry. These are essentially non-durable products, designed to last a limited amount of time with a limited amount of use.

Quiltmakers and crafters are really giving a special application to a product that is actually designed for something else. It is unfortunate the information quilters need—to determine if the fabric they are purchasing is appropriate for their end use—is not readily available to them. Competition among fabric suppliers to supply fabric to us with the "look" they think we want does give us a wonderful variety to work with, but does not alter the fact that most of the fabric is manufactured to fashion specifications,

not artisan standards. We need to realize that a lot of cotton fabric on the market today will encourage polyester batting to beard, will fade drastically when exposed to sunlight, will gradually lose its color when laundered in water in which chlorine is present and/or when added with today's stronger detergents, and has the potential to unravel in a seam if it has a low thread count. Wouldn't it be helpful if the manufacturers had to post this information on the bolt boards? . . . if we had our own standards and guidelines for which fabrics were suitable for quiltmaking? Then consumers, especially quilters, could have specific guidelines about how to care for the fabrics and the quilts made from those fabrics, as well as realistic expectations about how the fabric would behave. I do not want to come across as implying that the fabrics are all bad, because they aren't. Properly used, these fabrics will produce wonderful quilts that will last for many years, perhaps decades. These fabrics will not, however, allow us to overlook poor quality for the sake of a pretty color or print, treat them carelessly, or let us disregard the information available here by assuming the industry is looking out for us. It is time to take responsibility for our fabrics.

I would urge everyone reading this book to learn, question, experiment, and find out all you can about how a fabric behaves before you spend valuable hours making a treasured quilt, only to have the fabric sabotage the project. The following chapters contain information to help you learn and understand more about today's fabrics.

The information given in this book is provided to help you understand why fabric does what it does. The standards and guidelines used in the production and sale of quality fabric at fair prices is not only the responsibility of manufacturers and converters, but also the retailers and consumers. Legislation can never replace informed buying. Therefore, the tests, along with the technical information given, will help you gain the knowledge necessary to make intelligent buying decisions when you are choosing fabrics.

In order to understand what cotton fabric is all about, let's start with its properties, where it comes from, how it is made into fabric, and what processes it withstands before it becomes available to us on the shelf in the local quilt shop or fabric store.

CHAPTER 2

COTTON

Mature cotton bolls

HISTORICAL REVIEW

The origin of cotton is unknown. Archaeologists suggest that cotton was raised in Egypt about 12,000 BC, but their information remains inconclusive. It is generally agreed that cotton was used in India around 3,000 BC and in Peru around 2,300 BC.

The culture of cotton in the United States dates back about 2,500 years. Fragments of cotton fabrics have been found in dry caves and burial sites of the Native Americans in Utah, Texas, and Arizona, indicating that it was grown there as early as 500 BC. Cultivation of the cotton plant for fiber use as a profit-making venture began between 1607 and 1620 in Virginia, where cotton was abundant. Records show that sufficient cotton was grown in Virginia and the Carolinas by 1700 to furnish clothing to one-fifth of the population of those states. As demand increased, the need to go inland with farming was necessary. Sea Island cotton, which thrived near the coast, would not tolerate the inland climate. Upland varieties were necessary for these new climates. This caused a problem,

as the only gin available at the time, the Churka, imported from India, would only gin Sea Island cotton. Eli Whitney invented a saw-type gin in 1793, allowing the production of Upland cotton to increase rapidly.

The economic and social effects of this new gin were revolutionary. The increase in cotton production and consequent development of low-cost textiles led directly to the industrialization of both Europe and America. This fostered the massive export-import business between the two continents, and indirectly led to the overwhelming resurgence of slavery, which before this time was dying out, but was stimulated by the onset of the southern cotton culture.

Originally the factories for manufacturing and processing cotton into yarns and fabrics were located mostly in the New England states because of an abundant supply of water, power, and labor. The first spinning mill was opened in the United States in 1791. By 1810 there were 226 mills in the New England area. The Civil War changed this, however. With the change in

FROM FIBER TO FABRIC

the economy, manufacturing needed to be closer to the fiber supply source in the south. The move to the south reduced transportation costs and taxes, as well as providing plants with plentiful and cheap labor. Another very important reason for the move was that prior to the invention of air conditioning and humidity control, only the New Bedford and Providence, Rhode Island, location had the proper humidity conditions for cotton yarn spinning. This is a very critical factor. If the air is too humid, cotton will stick during spinning. If the air is too dry, the yarns will not form. The combination of moderate humidity and non-union labor brought the entire textile industry south in the early 1900s.

Fragments of cotton fabrics have been found in dry caves and burial sites of the Native Americans in Utah, Texas, and Arizona, indicating that it was grown there as early as 500 BC.

Cotton yarn and fabric manufacturing still remains a major business in the southern states of the United States, with North Carolina the nation's number one state in primary textile employment and production. There are about 1,000 textile manufacturing facilities in North Carolina, and about 6,000 nationwide. The production of cotton has increased over the years through improved farming techniques. More cotton of better quality is produced on less acreage than ever before.

COTTON FIBER PROPERTIES

Fiber Length

Depending on the variety, cotton fiber length varies from 0.9 inch to about 1.6 inches. The majority of the cotton grown in the United States is Upland. It has a fineness (diameter) of 18 microns (18/1,000 of a millimeter) and an average length of 1.1 inches. Long staple cotton has a fineness (diameter) of less than 15 microns and an average length of over 1.125 inches long. In the United States this cotton is produced mainly in the southwest. It is sold under the names of Pima or Supima cotton. Long staple cotton is produced in small quantities due to the high cost of growing and processing it.

Physical Characteristics

Cotton is a highly crystalline material. It burns or chars before it melts. When exposed to water (or steam) it swells, and upon drying, returns to the configuration in which it was dried. A quick shot of steam from a steam iron can reconstitute the cotton fiber.

Because consumers require modern cotton fabrics to deter wrinkling, many of today's fabric finishes, such as "durable press" or "wrinkle free," permanently set the cloth in a specific configuration. The term commonly used in the industry for these finishes is CRF (crease-resistant finish). These finishes cause reduced strength and abrasion resistance. This reduction in strength is balanced out at the mill by an increase in raw material strength before the CRF treatment is applied. For example: tensile strength of forty pounds before treatment will be thirty to thirty-five pounds after treatment. The mill, then, will start with forty-five to fifty pounds instead of forty pounds.

Absorbency

Cotton has the ability to absorb moisture, a major factor in its comfort. It can pick up about four percent of the moisture from the air. This allows it to conduct static electricity somewhat, and reduces "clinging." You might see it cling when it is bone dry, just out of the dryer, but with exposure to humid air it quickly loses its static electricity.

Stability

Cotton fibers themselves are relatively stable and do not stretch or shrink. Cotton fabrics, however, do shrink as a result of tensions applied during yarn and fabric construction. The industry has therefore tried to make the fabrics shrink resistant so the fabric remains stable during use and care.

Durability

Cotton fabrics decompose gradually with long exposures to dry heat and become brittle in extreme cold. Cotton will also deteriorate from mildew, which results in rotting and loss of strength. Moths do not damage cotton, but silverfish will eat cotton.

COTTON'S POPULARITY AND AVAILABILITY

Worldwide, cotton is still the most widely used fiber. The cost of cotton fabrics depends on several factors, including the quality and quantity of the crop (weather, pests, etc.), printing and finishing processes, chemicals used, equipment costs, and labor costs, as well as light or heavy demand for goods by the consumer.

CHAPTER 3

FROM FIBER TO FABRIC

Photo: Harriet Hargrave

A cotton stripper

GROWTH AND PRODUCTION

The cotton plant is a member of the same family as the hibiscus and hollyhock. It grows most successfully in warm climates where rain or irrigation can provide sufficient water when needed.

The plant blooms about one hundred days after planting. The petals drop off after forty-eight hours, leaving the boll, or seed pod, where the fibers form. Fifty to eighty days later the pod bursts open, and the soft cotton fibers are ready for picking. The modern cotton plant is a miracle of genetic engineering by "seed breeders." The size, amount, location on the plant, and maturity date of the cotton is controlled by genetics designed into the plant. Also, the length, strength, and fineness of the fiber are genetically controlled.

Before picking, the plants are often sprayed with defoliants. These sprays cause the leaves to shrivel and fall off. As the cotton bolls mature and open, the cotton fibers appear as fluffy white puffs.

Cotton Picking and Stripping

Cotton is picked by machine, using either a picker or a stripper. A picker pulls the fibers from the open bolls and is best used on fields with lush growth and high yield. It picks two to four rows at a time and can go over the field several times if needed. Strippers pull the entire boll from the plant, and are most effective on fields with low yields and low-growing plants. They pull from two to four rows simultaneously and go over a field only once.

Mature cotton boll with fibers ready for picking

FROM FIBER TO FABRIC

Hand picking was once the only way to harvest cotton. It produced the most uniform and best quality fiber. However, because of high labor costs and inadequate labor available, the use of hand pickers in the United States is now nonexistent. Seed breeders have made the cotton plant machine harvestable.

Cotton Ginning

After the cotton has been picked, it is taken to the gin. Here the fiber, called cotton lint, is separated from the seed. Today's gins, except for size, are principally the same as the first saw gin developed by Eli Whitney in 1793.

Not only is the lint separated from the seed in the gin, but foreign matter such as dirt, twigs, leaves, and parts of the boll are also removed. The seeds are a valuable byproduct of the cotton industry. Cattle feed and cottonseed oil are produced from these seeds. The fibers are packed into large bales weighing about five-hundred pounds.

Fiber Classification

Fiber class is determined by removing samples of the fibers from the bales. Classification is made using the following factors: staple

Cotton bales ready for shipment to textile mills

length, fiber grade, and character. *Staple length* is the length of the lint (fiber) and is often determined by the variety of the cotton plant. *Fiber grade* depends on color, amount

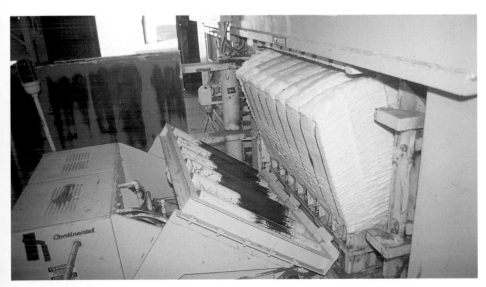

Modern cotton gin

of foreign matter present, and ginning preparation. The color can vary from white to gray to yellow. Mechanically picked fibers can have a lot of foreign matter, depending on picking conditions and weather. In mechanical harvesting, spotted or tinged cotton results because bolls that have been opened for some time are mixed with newly opened bolls. Hand-picked cotton, on the other hand, has very little foreign matter because the cotton is harvested at the time when the boll is mature. Fiber grade involves fiber fineness, color, and foreign matter. *Fiber character* includes fiber strength, uniformity, cohesiveness, pliability, elastic recovery, fineness, and resilience. When all this information has been gathered, the final quality of the cotton is established and a price is determined. Next, the fiber is baled and shipped to manufacturers of yarns and fabrics.

COTTON PROCESSING

To turn fibers into fabrics, the fibers are first converted into yarns, which are then woven into fabrics.

Once the bales arrive at the mill, the fibers from several different bales are combined. Cotton is opened in large opening and cleaning hoppers. Thin layers of fibers from different bales are fed into the blending machine.

These machines loosen and separate the tufts of closely packed fibers and remove stems, leaves, seed fragments, dirt, and other heavy impurities. This makes a uniform, well-blended mix. After several stages of opening and cleaning, the cotton lint is transported by air flow through large ductwork systems to "chutes" which uniformly feed the raw stock (lint) to the cards.

Opening process where fibers from bales are fluffed and blended

Opening and blending machine

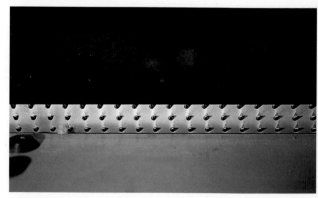

Close-up of metal fingers that pull tufts of fibers from bales to free them for processing

Carding

Carding continues the cleaning process, removing fibers too short for yarns, and separating and straightening the fibers so they lay parallel to each other. These fibers are then spread into a thin, uniform web. The web moves into a funnel-shaped device (trumpet) where it is gathered into a rope-like mass and formed into the *card sliver*.

Sliver being fed to drawing machine

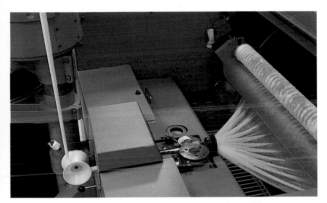
Layers of fibers from carding frame being gathered into card sliver

Breaker-drawing unit. The carded slivers are smoothed, drawn, and re-formed into one new sliver.

Combing

Combing is used for high-quality yarns of great evenness, smoothness, fineness, and strength. This operation combines several card slivers which are drawn into the comber and, once again, spread into a web. The fibers continue to be cleaned and straightened as the web is formed. Short fibers and all residual non-lint material are removed. This combed sliver is used to make high quality yarns.

Close-up of trumpet on carding frame

Depending on the quality of yarn being made, the sliver either goes to the drawing machine or the combing machine. Fine-quality cottons require yarns to be combed in addition to carding. The card sliver goes through the breaker-drawing step and then the combing operation.

Combing frame. Layers of fibers are fed to the combing area.

Drawing

Drawing follows either carding or combing, depending on the quality of yarn desired. Several strands of sliver (typically eight to ten) from different carding machines are combined and conveyed to the drawing machine, where they are pulled together and drawn out into a new sliver no larger than one of the original single slivers. The loose, rope-like strand of fibers resulting from this process is called **drawn sliver**.

Close-up of comb sliver ready for drawing frame

Today's mills use either two-process or three-process drawing, which describes the number of such processes of drawing that the sliver undergoes. The purpose of drawing is to make yarn more uniform by combing and elongating multiple slivers, thus eliminating the randomly occurring defects. After three processes of combining and drawing ten ends, random defects are virtually eliminated.

After drawing, rotor yarns go directly to the spinning frame. Ring spun yarns, however, must undergo an additional intermediate step between sliver and yarn called roving.

Roving

The drawn sliver is taken to the roving frame, where it is further drawn out until it measures from $1/8$ to $3/16$ inches in diameter. As the roving strand is ready to leave the roving frame, a slight twist is imparted to hold the fibers together.

Roving frame. Roller area reduces the diameter of drawn sliver as it moves between the rollers and comes out as roving.

Close-up of rollers on roving frame

Spinning

The final process in making the yarns is the actual spinning operation. The spinning frame converts the roving to a spun single yarn.

Spun yarns are composed of short lengths of fiber twisted or spun to hold them together. These short fibers are called staple fibers. The fibers are first processed to make them parallel, then alternately pulled and twisted. Other types of yarns include long staple (wool, linen, and acrylic) and continuous filament (acetate, nylon, silk, polyester, etc.).

Over the past twenty years cotton processing has changed. The two most widely used processes for making cotton yarn are ***ring spinning*** and ***rotor spinning***. Ring spinning is used for high-quality, smaller yarns (shirtings); rotor spinning is typically used for larger yarns (denim). Most combed yarns are ring spun.

Roving is drawn out into fine-spun yarn in spinning zone.

In ring spinning the roving is further drawn out to the desired diameter of the final yarn. The high-twist characteristic of spun yarns is added during this operation. This is where the term ring spinning comes in. In ring spinning, the drawn-out roving is guided downward through a small inverted U-shaped device called a traveler.

Spinning frame

The purpose of drawing is to make yarn more uniform by combing and elongating multiple slivers, thus eliminating the randomly occurring defects.

Close-up of traveler

rotor yarn is then pulled from the rotor. This too produces a single yarn. In some cases fine single yarns are combined into pairs called 2-ply yarns. The term *ply* indicates the number of single yarns twisted together to form a plied yarn, or the number of plied yarns twisted together to form cord. Plying is the twisting together of two or more single yarns or ply yarns to form, respectively, ply yarn or cord.

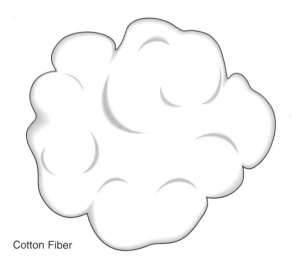
Cotton Fiber

The completed yarn is wound onto a spindle which rotates up to 13,000 revolutions per minute. If the speed of the traveler is too great, or if the edges are rough, the result will be frayed or hairy yarns, which will make fuzzy fabric and will cause pilling in cotton/polyester blends. The traveler moves around the ring at a rate of between 4,000 and 12,000 revolutions per minute. As the spindle revolves to wind the yarn, the yarn passes through the traveler, which carries it around the ring. This process gives the desired amount of twist and creates a single yarn.

In rotor spinning, the sliver is fed to a combing roll, which removes more or less individual fibers from the sliver and propels them into a rotor. This is very similar to a cotton candy machine, but the rotors are small and run at very high speed (20,000–60,000+ rpm). The

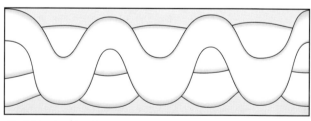
Straightening/drawing

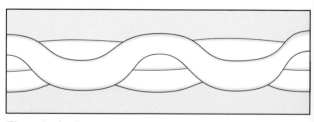
Elongating/roving

Single ply

1   2   3

3-ply yarn

Winding

Yarn from the spinning frame is next wound onto large spools or packages in a process called **winding**. These spools or packages are now used in weaving, knitting, and other operations. In some cases, packages of yarn may be dyed prior to knitting or weaving. This allows colored patterns to be produced in the fabric.

Weaving

Woven fabrics consist of two sets of yarns interlaced at right angles in established sequences. The yarns that run parallel to the selvage, or the length of the bolt of fabric, are called the warp yarns; those running the crosswise direction are called filling yarns.

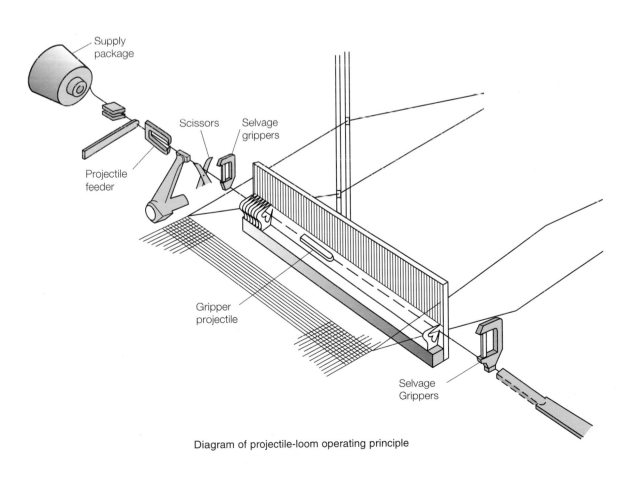

Supply package

Scissors

Selvage grippers

Projectile feeder

Gripper projectile

Selvage Grippers

Diagram of projectile-loom operating principle

Fabrics are identified by their construction. For example, 68 x 68 printcloth has 68 single-ply warp yarns per linear inch and 68 single-ply filling yarns per linear inch.

Yarns can be loosely or tightly woven. When the warp yarns equal the filling yarns in number per linear inch it is called a balanced (or square) fabric construction.

While several factors contribute to the quality of a fabric (the type of fibers used to make the yarn, the process taken to create and print the fabric, and the intended use of the fabric), **thread count** is a very useful way to describe a fabric. Determining the number of yarns per inch in both the warp and filling directions gives some information concerning how close the yarns are in each direction, as well as information on the appearance, flexibility, compactness, density, and performance of a woven fabric.

For many quilters the preferred yarn count is 68 x 68. 60 x 60 is beefier, but the lower yarn count uses fatter yarns to fill in the spaces. This makes a heavier, coarser fabric that ravels more easily, making it somewhat more difficult to work with. A smooth longer fiber makes finer yarns and thus finer cloth. In terms of appearance, the higher-count cloth provides sharper images of prints. The quality of materials we put into our quilts directly affects the final outcome.

The fabrics used in quiltmaking are mainly plain weave fabrics. Plain weave is the simplest and most used form of weaving. It consists of alternate interlacing of warp and filling yarns. These fabrics are reversible except for special finishes, prints, or other surface designs that give a right side to the fabric.

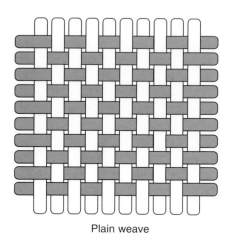

Plain weave

Cotton sateen fabric is a durable cotton fabric with a satin weave. Instead of interlacing alternate yarns, the warp yarns "float" over or under a predetermined number of filling yarns. These long floats give a lustrous look to the fabric.

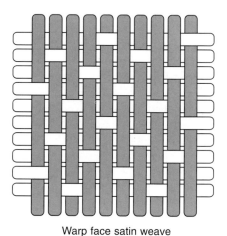

Warp face satin weave

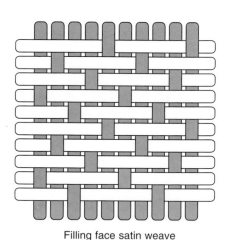

Filling face satin weave

CHAPTER 4

TEXTILE
PREPARATION

The fabric we see in retail stores goes through several steps before it is made available to the consumer. In Chapter 3 we discussed the making of cloth and different types of weaves used in quiltmaking fabric. But who determines the design, quality, and thread count of these fabrics?

A *converter* is an individual or organization that buys greige goods (usually directly from the mills), has the fabric dyed or printed and finished by other companies, and then sells the finished fabric. *Greige goods* (pronounced "gray" goods) are the unfinished fabrics in their raw state. All aspects of the fabric, including construction, design, color, and finish, are determined by the converter's specifications. The converters are generally much smaller than the large textile mills.

Companies such as P & B Textiles, Concord Fabrics, Inc., Benartex, and VIP are straight converters. They determine what quality greige goods they will use, buy them, and have a contractual relationship with the mill or finisher they use. They provide the printworks with the designs and colors to be printed. A company that produces and finishes fabric in its own plant is an integrated converter. Springs Mills is an integrated converter.

When we look at fabrics in the retail arena, we often see the same print on different greige goods. This happens when a converter buys a collection of designs from the plant and determines what quality cloth to print on, taking into consideration his market and price point. Obviously, if he wants to sell the fabric for a low price, he needs to print on lower quality greige goods and/or use less costly, lower-quality dyes and finishes. He could also print the same design on higher-quality cloth, use higher-quality dyes and finishes, and charge a higher price. It just depends on the market the mill or converter is targeting. Since converters sell their finished fabrics to the same customers as the mills, it is easy to see why so many qualities are available, and how confusing it can be for consumers.

FABRIC PREPARATION

Before any dyeing or printing can be done, preparation processes are undertaken to purify and rid the fabric of all soil and additives used during the weaving processes. These processes are the first treatments a fabric undergoes after leaving the loom, and are required before any dyeing or printing can be accomplished. PFD stands for prepare for dye and PFP stands for prepare for print.

At this point the fabric is referred to as greige goods. Greige goods are loom state fabrics that are not ready to be printed. They are in their "raw" state. Greige goods come in many different qualities and from many different countries. Many factors contribute to high- or low-quality greige goods.

- Quality of the raw cotton (good crop vs. bad crop)
- Length of the staple fiber (Pima (long) vs. Upland (short))
- Yarn used in weaving (the weight, grade, and character of yarn)
- Thread (yarn) count (the number of yarns per linear inch in the warp and filling directions)

Greige goods contain oils, waxes, and other foreign matter, commonly called "trash," as well as dirt and soil picked up during processing. Various types of cleaning processes are used.

The first step is to make a continuous rope of fabric from the bales of yardage that are shipped into the plant. Workers join the ends of

Greige goods room. Bales of greige goods are stitched together in preparation for cleaning.

each piece with a machine that resembles a serger. These ladder seams are often seen in bolts of fabric at the store. It is critical that not one of these ends is missed. The rope of fabric is several miles long, and is threaded through a maze of guides and machines. It often goes up three floors and back down again, from building to building, during the cleaning process. If an end is missed, the rope is broken, and the entire system has to be "rethreaded."

Singeing

Singeing is an important part of pretreatment. This is the burning off of protruding fiber ends from the surface of the fabric. If this is not done properly, unclear print patterns, mottled fabric surfaces, and pilling results. First the fabric surfaces are brushed lightly to raise the unwanted fiber ends, then the fabric is singed with heated plates or open flames. As soon as the fabric leaves the singeing area, it enters a desizing bath. This stops any singeing afterglow or sparks that might damage the cloth.

Approach to singeing room

Open flame singeing

Desizing

Desizing is a process which removes the chemical stiffener (a starch or other stiffener) applied to warp yarns to make them easier to weave. In some cases this starch (or stiffener) can be recycled and returned by tanker trucks to weaving plants. Natural oils, waxes, and man-made lubricants are removed by caustic (or alkali) agents. Desizing also softens and removes any trash particles and seed-coat fragments. The desizing bath is a bath of enzymes that saturate the cloth. The cloth continues through additional baths containing more enzymes and detergents that loosen the sizing present and prepare the fabric for the scouring and bleaching. Cloth moves through the singeing and desizing process at a rate of up to 300 yards per minute.

Bleaching

Bleaching is required to obtain pure whites, since fibers are seldom pure white in their natural state. The bleaches are chemical agents that react with the color compounds in the fiber and render them colorless. Bleaching is a very important step in obtaining the desired end product. If the fabric is not properly bleached during preparation, it may retain its natural color, which would distort the color of the fabric when dyes or pigments are added. Fabrics with bright, even, rich color must be pure white to begin with. Cotton is bleached with 10% chlorine compounds and/or 90% hydrogen peroxide. Following the bleaching process the fabric is put through a final washing to remove all the chemicals, and a final rinse to completely free the fabric of all chemicals used in these processes.

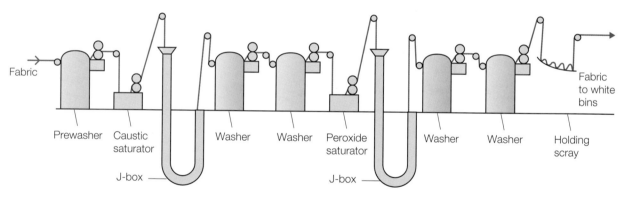

Basic steps in rope bleaching and scouring

Rope bleaching range

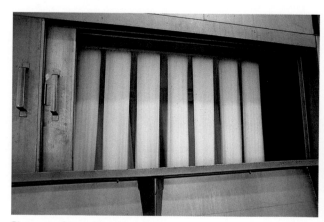

Close up of rope bleaching range

Mercerization

Mercerization is a chemical treatment (caustic soda) applied to cellulose fibers, especially cotton. It adds luster to fabric, improves dyeing characteristics, and increases strength. The cotton fiber cross section is kidney-bean shaped before treatment. Mercerization swells the cotton fiber (cross section) to a round shape. Cotton left in its original shape reflects light unevenly. Mercerized cotton reflects light evenly and creates a gloss or sheen.

The natural crystallinity of cotton fiber is altered during mercerization. The fibers now have increased strength and increased affinity for dyestuffs, as well as increased luster.

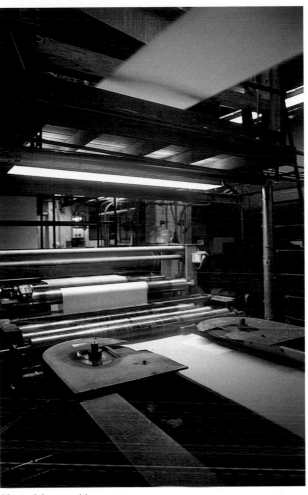
Mercerizing machine

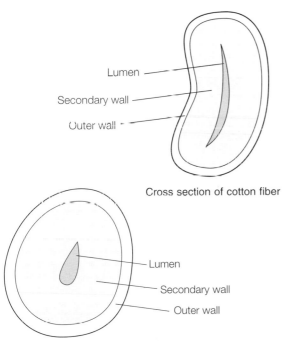

Cross section of cotton fiber

Cross section of mercerized cotton fiber

Tentering

Tentering is the mechanical straightening and drying of fabrics to secure uniform width and to keep the filling yarns on-grain. Why do fabrics need to be tentered? Fabric goes through a lot of stress during preparation, dyeing, printing, and finishing. This often causes

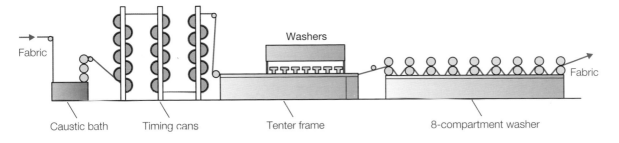

Basic steps of mercerization

the warp and filling threads to be off-grain. Tentering establishes the alignment of these warp and filling yarns. Properly tentered fabrics will be straight. This means that the warp and filling yarns are at 90° angles to one another. A tenter frame holds the fabric between two parallel chains, with either clips (tenters) or pins, while adjusting the side-to-side alignment of the cloth.

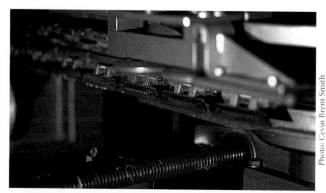

Tenter chain on tentering frame

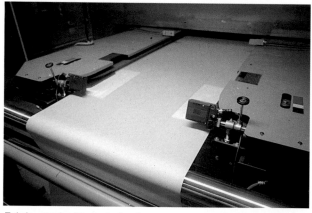

Fabric attached to tentering frame

The chains spread apart to the desired fabric width, move with the fabric through drying units, and release the fabric to the next process. This process is used after several of the finishing operations. If the fabric is fed to the chains so that the yarns are perpendicular, the fabric stays on-grain. If not, a bow or skew situation develops. Bow or skew tentering during the application of prints or colors produces fabric

that will cause problems for the consumer. We see this problem frequently with printed plaids and prints with a directional design. The fabric grain is straight, but the design is not.

With **bowed** fabric the filling yarns curve in the fabric and do not go straight across. It is caused by improper tenter frame procedures, sometimes the result of the frame operating at too high a speed. Bowed fabrics are especially serious in plaid, check, or striped fabrics, because they prevent proper joining of the pattern.

With **skewed** fabric the filling yarns are straight, but do not run perpendicular to the fabric edges (selvages). Both bowed and skewed fabrics are defective, and you should refuse to buy them.

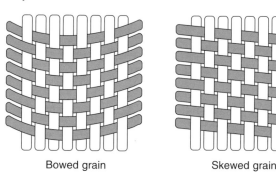

Bowed grain   Skewed grain

To test for these problems, simply lay a straight yardstick across the width of the goods. If the fabric is torn, it will tear with the yarn and show the defect readily. If cut, look at the threads as they lay along the yardstick. Find one yarn and follow it across the full width of the cloth. The yarn should not vary more than $3/8$" from the straight edge on 45"-wide goods. Fortunately, sensors at the mills have been developed to reduce the frequency of these problems. These sensors stop the machine as soon as yarns are not in their proper alignment, and stop or slow one chain until the grain is in alignment again.

Once the cloth is prepared, the fabric is sent to the dyehouse or printhouse, where the fabric is dyed and/or printed.

CHAPTER 5

TEXTILE
DYEING

Dyeing can be done during any stage of the textile manufacturing process. The fiber, the yarn, the fabric, or the finished piece can be dyed. In the case of 100% cotton fabrics, most dyeing is done as yarn or fabric, although garment dyeing has recently gained in popularity.

There are several ways dyes are applied to commercially-made cloth. The two methods most frequently used on quilting fabrics are batch (exhaust) and continuous.

BATCH DYEING

Batch dyeing involves the use of complex chemical dyestuffs which, under proper conditions, will actually combine with the textile fiber molecule. In batch (exhaust) dyeing, the fiber, yarn, or garment is immersed in a dye solution, using carefully regulated chemicals and temperatures. A specific quantity of fabric is loaded, and the dye chemically bonds with the fabric due to its natural affinity. (Affinity is a chemical attraction: the tendency of two elements or substances to unite or combine, such as fiber and dyestuff.) The dyestuff leaves the dye solution and attaches to the fiber over a period of minutes or hours. This action is accelerated and optimized by the use of chemicals and controlled temperatures. Once in the fiber, the dye is fixed in place, and then the textile is washed.

CONTINUOUS DYEING

Continuous dyeing is accomplished by passing the fabric in a flat open-width manner through a series of rollers and processing baths in a large machine containing various chemical solutions, heated ovens, steamer sections, and the like. The same types of dyes may be used for continuous dyeing as are used for batch dyeing described above.

Continuous Application of Pigments

Another continuous method uses pigments. These are colorants with no particular affinity for the fabric or fiber; instead they are held in place by binders. It is similar to painting a surface with latex paints. Pigment dyeing or tinting involves a controlled application of the pigment and binder mixture. In pigment dyeing, the application is uniform. In pigment printing, the application is localized. In either case, this is followed by high-temperature drying.

Pigment dyed or printed fabric often has only moderate durability to washing and crocking (rubbing), since the pigments reside on the surface of cloth. The binders and other auxiliary chemicals used are a means to ensure fastness qualities. In most cases they work in conjunction with heat to impart crock- and washfastness properties to the pigment dyes being applied to the fabric. The colorfastness depends largely on the pigment binder used. Sometimes pigment-dyed fabric can be identified because dark colors do not look rich, but flat and chalky, and have a stiff hand.

The Differences Between Continuous and Batch Dyeing

Comparing the two, continuous dyeing costs less for long runs (typically over 10,000 yards) in terms of labor, water, and waste. But for short runs (typically under 1,000 yards) the reverse is true.

Consumers are usually more concerned with choosing the right color than they are with selecting fabrics that provide durability and good performance.

In continuous dyeing, dye fixation is accomplished with steam, dry heat, or chemical reaction, and the ovens, steamers, and chemical pads in the continuous operation require close attention and optimization for each recipe. The quality of continuous-dyed fabric is equal to or better than batch-dyed fabric because high affinity, which is so important in batch dyeing, is not required for continuous dyeing. Pigments used in the continuous process use binders to physically hold onto the textile, much as paint holds onto a wall. Pigments have no natural ability to integrate with the fiber whereas fiber reactive, vat, Napthols and disperse dyesuffs do. In continuous dyeing, some high affinity dyes cause problems such as *tailing* (when individual colors separate out of solution causing unevenness of color) and difficult washing, thus requiring excessive water. However, continuous dyeing is generally less polluting than batch for longer runs.

OTHER TYPES OF DYEING

Yarn Dyeing

Yarn dyeing is the dyeing of yarns before they have been woven into fabrics. Yarns may be dyed in different forms: skeins, packages, or beams. Skein dyeing is immersing large, loosely wound hanks (skeins) of yarn in dye vats. Soft, lofty yarns such as hand knitting yarns are usually skein dyed.

Package Dyeing

Package dyeing uses yarn that is wound on small perforated tubes, called packages. Many packages fit into the dyeing machine, where the dye flows alternately from the center to the outside, then the outside to the center. These yarns are used to produce patterns in knitted and woven fabrics.

Package dyeing

Photo courtesy of Pendleton Woolen Mills

Beam Dyeing

Beam dyeing is simply a larger version of package dyeing. In beam dyeing an entire warp beam of warp yarn or woven fabric is wound onto a perforated cylinder made of wood or metal, which is placed in the beam dyeing machine. The dye is forced through the perforated cylinder from the inside out and from the outside in. The dye bath alternates the same as package dyeing.

Yarn dyeing is economical and provides good color absorption. The various colored yarns can be used in designing plaids, checks, stripes, and iridescent fabrics. Many of our homespuns and plaids are yarn dyed.

Piece Dyeing

Piece dyeing is the dyeing of cloth after it has been knit or woven. It is the most adaptable and lowest-cost method of dyeing fabrics a solid color.

Pad Dyeing

Pad dyeing is commonly used to dye cotton solids. The dyeing is done as part of a continuous dye range, where large quantities of fabric are continuously run through a pad, then into heat or steam chambers to set the dye, then into washers, rinsers, and dryers to finally emerge as completely dyed fabric.

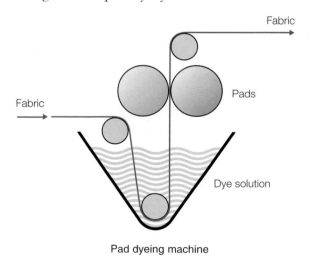

Pad dyeing machine

COLORFASTNESS OF DYES

Colorfastness refers to a color's permanence or its ability to remain unchanged throughout the useful life of the article to which it has been applied. Some colors may have excellent fastness to laundering, but poor fastness to sunlight. It is unfair to state that a color is simply fast or fugitive without qualifying to what it might be fast or fugitive.

No coloring agent used for textiles is absolutely fast to all conditions of use or environmental exposure.

Common environmental and use conditions that affect the fastness of color are: sunlight, different laundry products, dry cleaning, abrasion (also known as crocking), perspiration, swimming pool water, bleach (chlorine), pollutants, and gases in the atmosphere. Many of these conditions can be tested by the quiltmaker at home to see if the fabric in question is suitable for the desired end use. These tests will be discussed in Chapter 8.

TYPES OF DYES

There are many types of dyes, classified according to the type of fibers to which they apply, or by the dyeing class itself. Cotton dyes include direct, fiber reactive, vat, azoic, mordant, and sulfur dyes.

Not all dyes are capable of combining with all textile fibers. For example, some dyes will combine with protein (wool) fibers and not with cellulose (cotton) fibers. When a particular dye is capable of combining with a fiber and can permanently impart color to it, we say that the dye has an affinity for that fiber. The basis for classifying dyes is their ability to impart color—regardless of whether or not a chemical reaction between the dye and a fiber takes place. Most dyes within each class possess similar, but not necessarily equal, fastness characteristics. Pigments, being held in place by binders, apply equally well (or poorly) to all fibers. The affinity of many dye-fiber combinations does not rely on chemical bonding as much as it relies on mechanical entrapment and/or solubility of the dye when in the fiber.

The following chart shows the percentages of each dye used in quiltmaking fabrics today:

AZOIC	Cotton, cellulosic	9%
DIRECT	Cotton, rayon, cellulosic	31%
FIBER REACTIVE	Cotton, cellulosic, wool, rayon	32%
MORDANT (obsolete)	Natural fibers (pretreat w/ metals)	0%
SULFUR	Cotton, other cellulosic	7%
VAT	Cotton, other cellulosic	21%

Azoic Dyes

Azoic dyes (also called Napthol) produce color as a result of a chemical action in the fiber between a diazotized amine and a coupling agent. Azoic dyes produce bright or brilliant colors such as deep reds, violet, and burgundy shades, as well as yellows and oranges. They have excellent colorfastness to washing and are relatively low in cost, but can vary from good to poor in light and chlorinefastness. Heavier (darker) colors can have problems with crocking (rubbing).

Direct Dyes

Direct dyes are one of the largest groups of dyes. They are applied by dissolving the dyestuff in a water bath, and adding a salt to control the absorption rate of the dye by the fiber. The fabric is then immersed in the dyebath. The amount of dyestuff absorbed depends on the size of the dye molecule and the size of the pore opening in the outer surface of the fiber. Direct dyes have moderate fastness to washing. The fastness to light varies but some are excellent and used in drapery and upholstery. Fastness to dry cleaning is good to excellent.

Fiber Reactive Dyes

Fiber reactive dyes actually react chemically with the cotton fiber molecule, producing a high degree of colorfastness. Fiber reactive dyes will produce bright clean colors. They generally have good to excellent fastness to laundering, crocking, and dry cleaning, and poor to high fastness to light, but can be sensitive to chlorine. The major drawback is cost. These dyes can cost anywhere from thirty to sixty cents more per yard to produce. By the time the fabric gets to the consumer, this could mean an increase of $2.00/yard or more.

Sulfur Dyes

Sulfur dyes are used mainly for black, but also for deep shades such as navy and brown. They have excellent fastness to light and washing, but poor fastness to chlorine. Some sulfur dyes cause tendering (weakening) of fabric if stored for great lengths of time under warm, humid conditions.

Vat Dyes

Vat dyes have excellent fastness to light and washing, and are very fast to chlorine and other oxidizing bleaches. However, they may crock if improperly applied. Indigo denim is an example of a vat-dyed textile.

OTHER COLORANTS

Pigments are completely different substances for coloring textiles. Pigments, unlike dyes, are coloring agents which are insoluble in water, and do not unite or combine in any way with the textile fiber. Pigment particles are microscopic-sized, colored chips which are held on the surface of a fiber by binding agents. The color is mixed with a binder and applied as a binder/pigment mixture. Pigments cannot be applied to fibers or yarns, but only to fabrics as solid color or as prints. Solid colors are applied by the pad method. They must be forcibly squeezed into the cloth so the inside fibers will be colored. The binder/pigment is applied, then heat cured. This involves heating the fabric to 300°–400°F for thirty seconds to several minutes. This is known as curing, and renders the binder permanent.

Pigments are economical and come in a wide variety of colors. They also have very good lightfastness, but rubbing (crocking) and washing can accelerate color loss and fading. Oftentimes the binders tend to stiffen the cloth, which can be a problem in some end uses, but new finishes are counteracting this problem more and more.

As to the durability of any of these colorants, most textile operations have a quality control laboratory that ensures the fabric leaving that particular plant will pass specifications outlined by the customer (converter).

As a consumer it is very difficult, if not impossible, to tell what type of dye was used to color a fabric. There are some fairly simple tests that will be discussed in Chapter 8 that can assist you in identifying specific dyes or pigments. Azoic dye is often the only dye that will give the strength and brilliancy of a desired color. Fiber reactive dyes can produce most colors, but the higher cost is a factor. Pigments give a huge variety of color and are very lightfast, but do not launder well over time. The issue for quilters is which dyes will prolong the life of the quilt? If the quilt is going to be hung, lightfastness is very important and any of the dyes, except for azoic dyes, would be suitable. If the quilt will be used on a bed and washed frequently, then vat, fiber reactive, and azoic dyes are most suitable. As you can see, the end use of a fabric can dictate what dye should be used. Therefore, it is very important that quilters learn to test their fabric to make sure it can stand up to the wear the quilt will incur.

CHAPTER 6

TEXTILE
PRINTING

For printing, the fundamentals of dyestuffs, fabrics, and fastness properties are similar to dyeing. The process of printing is the localized application of color. This requires careful preparation of the cloth to provide optimum absorption of the print paste, without spreading. The print paste must be formulated to ensure proper flow during application, but also to stay in place until the fabric is dried. Commercially-printed cottons use Napthol (azoic) and fiber reactive dyes, and pigments. Refer to Chapter 5 for specific characteristics of each of these dyes.

Dyes used in dyeing are usually put into a dye/water solution. When the same dyes or pigments are used for printing, they must be thickened with gums or starches to prevent wicking and flowing of the print design. This thickened solution is the consistency of thick mayonnaise and is called **print paste**. The print paste is a material that is actually on the surface of the fabric. Because of the base, it can melt when subjected to an iron that is too hot.

The two common methods for printing fabric are the roller print method and the screen print method.

ROLLER PRINTING

Roller printing accounts for about one-half of the printing done worldwide, but less than one-fourth of printing in the United States. Use of this method is decreasing, however, due to the difficulties and expense.

In roller printing the design is put onto fabric by copper or steel engraved rollers. The artist's design is exactly engraved onto the roller using a pantograph.

Roller printing is a high-speed process which can produce up to 6,000 yards of printed fabric per hour. This speed is determined by the complexity of the pattern being printed. A complex pattern can be as slow as 3,000 yards per hour.

Roller printing gives the highest resolution and highest quality fine line details. Extremely precise detail can be engraved into rolls for roller printing, whereas screen printing generally does not have as fine a resolution. Roller printing is more costly, and rollers are much harder to make than screens.

The printing machine contains a series of engraved metal rollers positioned around a large padded cylinder. Most machines can accommodate rollers with up to a sixteen-inch circumference. This means the fabric cannot have a repeat spaced farther apart than sixteen inches. Most roller printing machines can accommodate up to eight rollers, but the use of more than four rollers is uncommon. A separate engraved roller is required for each color in the print. Excellent color definition can be achieved by rollers, but in some cases the addition of several colors can "crush" the color into the cloth.

When the rollers are mounted on the printing machine, they must be carefully adjusted within fractions of an inch to assure each color segment of a pattern is in its proper space on the printed material. This is called **registration**. Failure to do this will cause distortion of the print.

The rollers rotate in the print paste. The engraved patterns pick up the print paste and transport it to the fabric. Print paste is brushed on the rollers, then excess paste is removed by a "doctor blade," which removes the excess dye from the unengraved portion of the roller, leaving the engraving on the roller filled with printing paste. This is then transferred to the fabric. Each roller supplies one color to the finished design, and as the fabric passes between the roller and the padded cylinder, each color in the design is applied.

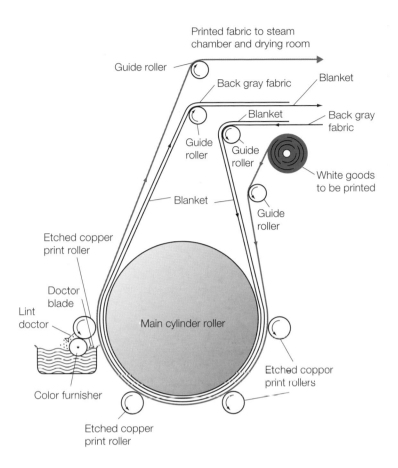

Printed fabric to steam
chamber and drying room

Guide roller

Back gray fabric

Blanket

Blanket

Back gray
fabric

Guide
roller

Guide
roller

White goods
to be printed

Blanket

Etched copper
print roller

Guide
roller

Doctor
blade

Lint
doctor

Main cylinder roller

Color furnisher

Etched coppor
print rollers

Etched copper
print roller

Basic steps in roller printing

Engraving of roller

Roller printing machine

TEXTILE PRINTING

39

SCREEN PRINTING

Screen printing is basically a refined stencil process. The screen is made by covering a flat frame, or by forming the screen into a closed cylinder with a fine-mesh fabric of silk, metal, nylon, or polyester filament. At one time the screens used for this process were made from fine silk yarns and the process was called silk-screen printing. The process is still often called silk-screening, but the screens are no longer made of silk. A film which has had the design areas etched out is placed over the screen. This leaves the mesh fabric open for the colorant to pass through. The print paste is forced from the interior of the screen onto the cloth in a rotary screen, or with a squeegee for flat bed printing.

The design is created when the print paste is allowed to pass through the design areas of the film and register as the printed pattern. There is a screen for each color to be used. Flat bed printing is time consuming and very expensive, but permits very large-scale patterns to be printed. While flat bed screens are still used in Japan, very few are still used in the United States.

Today most screen printing is done on a rotary screen. The screen is curved into a cylinder, and the dye is fed through the openings from the ends of the cylinder. The rotary screen is placed on a printing frame. This form of screen printing is continuous, as is roller printing.

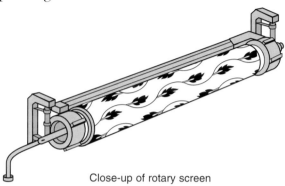

Close-up of rotary screen

Screen printing is used for the production of larger pattern repeats. Dyes or pigments are laid on top of the fabric, not crushed into the fabric as in roller printing. Screen printing can give the appearance of cleaner and brighter colors.

Many fabrics can be alternately produced with dyes or pigments. However, as with any variation in production, the colorfast properties can also vary.

Hand screen printing

FROM FIBER TO FABRIC

Screen printed fabric. White line indicates repeat.

Rotary screen printing

Fabrics printed with dyes (not pigments) are called wet prints. Once the fabric is printed, it must go through further treatment to set the color. The printed fabric is exposed to steam near or exceeding the boiling point. This step is called **aging**. Following aging, the fabric is passed through soap baths to remove the thickeners and other substances used in making the print paste. This is called **soaping**.

When pigments are used instead of dyes, it is referred to as pigment printing. The fabric is put through dry heat at temperatures of up to 400°F for several minutes to set the binder which holds the pigment. This is known as **curing**. The soaping process is unnecessary in pigment printing.

The printing of fabrics is a surface treatment. Unless the fabric is lightweight, the printed colors rarely penetrate into the fabric structure. Laundering, dry cleaning, and tumble drying, as well as abrasion from use, tend to wear off the surface fibers and result in a faded look. This wearing causes uncolored fibers to emerge on the fabric surface.

Fabrics that are subjected to heavy wear and cleanings fare better when yarn dyed or piece dyed rather than printed. These fabrics show the pattern equally well on the face and back, whereas printed fabrics only show the pattern well on the front.

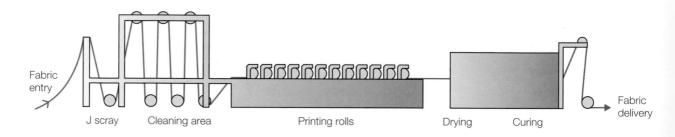

Basic steps in rotary screen printing

TYPES OF PRINTING

There are three basic types of prints that can be roller or screen printed: direct, discharge, and resist.

Direct Printing

With direct prints the design is printed directly onto a white cloth or previously dyed fabric. You can identify these fabrics because:

- the background is white or has large portions of white background;
- the printed design is lighter in shade on the back of the fabric than on the face; or

When a dyed fabric is used, the fabric is called an **overprint**. With an overprint, the background color is the same shade on the face and back and the print design is darker than the background.

Discharge Printing

With discharge prints fabrics are dyed prior to printing, then the design is applied with a chemical that bleaches out the color of the originally dyed fabric. One example is a white micro dot on a navy ground. The fabric is dyed navy, then the dots are "printed" with a chemical that takes away the navy color. You can identify these fabrics because:
- the background color is the same shade on the face and back of the cloth;
- the print design area is white or a different color than the background; or
- if you look closely at the back of the fabric, you can see traces of the original background color in the print design area.

Discharge printing is not widely used because production is more costly. The fabric must be dyed before printing, and very careful process controls are required. In recent years the development of automatic and rotary screen printing have produced high-quality blotch prints that have the same effect as discharge prints but at a lower cost.

Resist Printing

Resist prints are made by printing a design onto a white fabric with a chemical that prevents or "resists" the penetration of dyes. The fabric is then piece dyed. The result is a dyed background with a white patterned area. The look is similar to discharge prints, but the process is done in reverse. This is the method used to create batik prints. This method is not widely used in commercially-produced fabrics.

It is impossible to distinguish between discharge and resist prints, since both types of prints produce similar results.

By learning to identify different types of prints and learning about the pigments and dyes used to produce fabrics, you will become a better consumer, able to make informed decisions about your quilting projects.

PIGMENT PRINTS

Pigment prints are textile prints which are produced with pigments rather than with dyes. They are so widely used they have come to be regarded as a separate print-type category. The majority of domestically-made quilt fabrics are pigment prints because fiber reactive dyes are more expensive in the United States. Pigment prints are direct prints made with pigments. Depending on the binder, pigments can be identified by the difference in stiffness between the printed and nonprinted portions of the same fabric. A pigment printed area can be stiffer and a bit thicker than the nonprinted area. If the fabric was printed with dyes, there would be no discernible difference in stiffness between these two areas.

Deep shades of pigment are likely to be stiffer than light shades or pastels. White pigments are also used in the white-on-white prints so popular now. When testing a fabric, check all the colors because the same print may contain both dyes and pigments.

Pigment prints are the least costly type of print because they take the least amount of processing. They produce bright rich colors and have good lightfastness, but lose color and fade with rubbing and washing. This fading is caused by the gradual loss of resin binders from the agitation and tumbling action in laundering. The fabric will usually show distinct fading by about the fifteenth or twentieth washing. Dark shades show more color loss because they are not fast to crocking (rubbing).

By learning to identify different types of prints and learning about the pigments and dyes used to produce fabrics, you will become a better consumer, able to make informed decisions about your quilting projects. You will know what fabrics to look for when making an art piece for a wall in a bright room or a quilt you will sleep under every night.

CHAPTER 7

TEXTILE
FINISHES

BASIC FINISHES

Finishes are classified in various ways. They are applied by mechanical or chemical process, and each finish is classified as permanent, durable, semi-durable, or temporary.

Permanent finishes involve a chemical change in the fiber structure that will not change or alter throughout the life of the fabric. Durable finishes usually last the life of the article, but will lose their effectiveness slightly after each cleaning. Semi-durable finishes last for several cleanings, and temporary finishes are removed the first time they are laundered.

Quilters need to be aware that today's cottons are finished to allow the fabric to "relax" and let go of wrinkles. Our quilts, on the other hand, need knife-edge seams, especially for appliqué. How can a finish release wrinkles and still hold a press at the same time? It is obvious that many of the fabrics could work against us if we don't know what to expect. The following finishes are typically used on cottons.

It is obvious that many of the fabrics could work against us if we don't know what to expect.

MECHANICAL FINISHES

Calendering

Calendering is a temporary mechanical finish that smooths or flattens the surface of fabrics. It is much the same as ironing. When combined with some finishes it may be relatively durable, but calendering typically must be repeated following any application of moisture.

Glazing calendering produces a highly glazed, polished effect on one side of a fabric

Calendering machine

surface. Schreiner Calendering produces a low, soft-key luster on the fabric surface. Since the finish will easily wash out, resin treating before this processing occurs will result in greater durability of the finishing's effect. Resins produce a durable finish which usually lasts the life of the item. Resin treating fabrics is an established form of finish control. However, over-application of resins in conjunction with heat causes loss of tensile strength in the fabric. Polished cotton and chintz are quilting fabrics finished by glazing calendering. These substances fill the spaces between the yarns and are necessary to provide the glazed appearance.

- High-polish finishes can wash off and dull in water, but they do hold a crease if resin is incorporated in the finishing process. They are damaged by abrasion and the finish tends to rub off. The fabric can be brittle.

- Low-polish finishes lose their shine with washing, but regain a low luster when ironed. They are more wrinkle and abrasion resistant and are considered a durable to temporary finish, depending on whether the fabric is resin treated or not.

Chintzes were traditionally finished with a form of shellac. This finish was durable on the fabric and would not wash off for a long time. Most of today's chintzes are made in heavier decorator weights for upholstery, where stuffing eliminates the problem of wrinkles.

- Lightweight cotton chintzes are available but tend to have a high thread count, which makes hand quilting more difficult. They do work successfully with machine quilting.

- Polyester/cotton chintzes are good for whole-cloth quilts. These fabrics tend to be a bit heavier than most quilting cottons. The polyester fiber content makes piecing difficult, and the fabric may pill with use.

Napping

Flannel is created by a mechanical finishing process called napping. Napping is applied to fabric woven with staple fiber yarns to produce a raised surface nap.

Cloth used for napping is woven with soft-spun yarns that have a low twist and fairly loose fibers. Excellent results are obtained by using plain or twill weave fabrics. The warp yarns of these fabrics are strong and give the fabric strength. The filling yarns are loose and make napping easy.

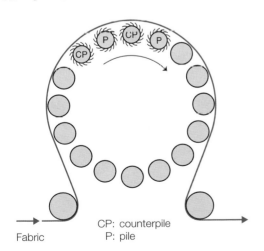

Diagram of the napping process. Fabric moves left to right, passing over napping rolls.

CP: counterpile
P: pile
Fabric

To achieve napping, the cloth is held under tension and passed through a napper as many as thirty times to obtain the desired amount of nap. A napper is a machine that uses cylinders of fine metal wires with small hooks, called raising rolls. There can be between twenty-four and thirty raising rolls evenly spaced around a large cylinder. Each raising roll is covered at 1 1/16" intervals with 1/2"-long wires set at a 45° angle to the surface of the cloth. Each roll is set so that the wires are at opposite angles of each other. These are called pile (P) and counterpile (CP) rolls.

The fiber ends are pulled to the surface of the fabric by these wires. The pile rolls create long nap fibers and the counterpile rolls create short nap fibers on the fabric surface. The amount of tension on the fabric and the number of times the fabric passes through the napper determine the specific amount of napping achieved.

Napping can be done on one or both sides of the cloth. Shrinkage in these fabrics is generally higher than in normal weaves and finishes due to the loose, low-twist filling yarns.

Sueding

Sueding (or sanding) is a fairly new process which uses a machine called a sander. The process yields a softer, more luxurious feel to the fabric.

FABRIC SHRINKAGE

Shrinkage is affected by fabric design, construction, yarn twist, and finishing. The decision of whether to preshrink or not is based on the individual's needs. In garment construction preshrinking results in a more compact material with greater elasticity and less distortion in the final garment. In garments shrinkage of 4% in wovens (6% in knits) can mean a decrease of one size since we are dealing with more yardage. In quiltmaking, however, the greater elasticity you get from preshrinking can make it more difficult to cut and machine piece those small pieces. The stiffness of the finishing resins gives added body and allows the fabrics to take a crisper press. If you do not preshrink your fabric, you have the option of washing it after it is finished, which would give more surface texture and added strength to the overall item.

Differential Shrinkage

One problem that is fairly common is *differential shrinkage*. This is where two fabrics with different finishes are sewn together. This presents a problem at seams where one fabric shrinks differently from the other. The result is puckering. This can also occur when sewing the same fabric in different orientations—one seam lengthwise and one seam crosswise. If a fabric shrinks different amounts in the warp and in the fill direction, the seam will pucker. In a quilt, because we are cutting small pieces, sewing them together with other fabrics, layering them with a batting and backing, then quilting it, no one small piece of fabric will

shrink more than the batting or backing fabric. In fact, the batting is the strongest determinant of shrinkage in a quilt, not the individual fabrics in the piecing. In Chapter 12 I will explain how to test this principle, and you will see that shrinkage control in quiltmaking is "night and day" to garment construction.

Compressive Shrinkage

Compressive shrinkage is a mechanical finishing process used to control relaxation shrinkage. It is the mechanical compressing of damp fabric lengthwise by overfeeding it onto a large roller covered by a blanket. Fabrics labeled Sanforized™ have met strict requirements which limit shrinkage to less than one percent in length and/or width. Many fabrics treated by this method carry no trademark. They are called "compacted." Compacting is a semi-permanent treatment applied by the mill to stabilize shrinkage. It gradually "relaxes out" of the cloth during washing but does slow down the process of residual shrinkage. Compacting is used extensively on low-quality knit fabrics, while Sanforizing is used more often on wovens and higher-quality knits.

Compressive shrinkage machine

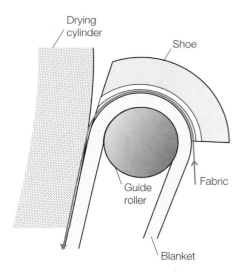

Drying cylinder

Shoe

Guide roller

Fabric

Blanket

Diagram of compressive shrinkage principle—Sanforizer

Photo: Cevin Brent Smith

Thermometer in vent tube of dryer

There are two other kinds of shrinkage in cottons: relaxation shrinkage and progressive shrinkage. **Relaxation shrinkage** is the shrinkage remaining in the fabric when it is purchased. It is the actual shrinkage that can occur during use and care. It occurs because the fibers and yarns are under great tension when the fabrics are made. Later, when the fabric becomes wet or steamed in a tensionless situation, the fabric draws up on itself—or relaxes. This type of shrinkage occurs only once. **Progressive shrinkage** is when the fabric continues to shrink wash after wash. It occurs when all potential shrinkage does not take place during the first laundering. This can be caused by various finishing agents, and as they are gradually removed additional shrinkage occurs.

CHEMICAL FINISHES

Durable press is a chemical treatment that stabilizes the fibers so they have a "memory" and return to the shape and configuration they were before treated. In durable press finishing the individual cotton fiber polymer (cellulose) molecules react with a cross-linking agent containing formaldehyde. Once this is done, water

Tumble dryers and dryer heat are large contributors to shrinkage in natural fabrics. Most shrinkage occurs when drying the last 25% of moisture out of the fabric. Shrinkage is also common in dryers with bad thermostats. It is very damaging and very dangerous to have a dryer that overheats. The temperature should never exceed 160°F (140°F is best). To test your dryer, put a dial thermometer (like an oven thermometer) in the exhaust vent tube, as close as possible to the drying chamber. At the end of the cycle, when the fabric is driest, the temperature will be highest. Check the temperature. If it is too hot, call the service technician for consultation immediately. If not repaired, the dryer could not only over-dry and over-shrink your clothes (especially knits and underwear), but also pose a serious fire hazard.

Tumble dryers are also culprits for color loss caused from crocking (friction) on pigment prints. If you choose to preshrink your print fabrics, consider line drying them, and pressing while damp with a perma-press setting on the iron. You will see little if any shrinkage, and a return of body to the fabric.

and other agents cannot swell or disrupt the fiber structure and the fabric is resistant to wrinkles and shrinking.

Scotchgard® is a chemical finish often discussed between quilters as to its appropriateness for our fabrics and quilts. Dr. Brent Smith, textile professor at North Carolina State University, said that Scotchgard, if properly applied (which it should be if applied at the factory), is a good thing. It makes the fabric more durable, lubricates the fabric, and makes it easier to sew and handle. It is less desirable, especially for very valuable items, when added afterward by the consumer. The advantages are fewer and there is a small risk of improper application, which could cause problems. The same warning applies to the 3M product called Zepel®.

There was a time when stored fabrics could release enough formaldehyde to give an objectionable odor, but that was in the 1960s and those days are long gone.

Formaldehyde

Free or unreacted formaldehyde is a product I am frequently asked about in lectures. There always seems to be fear about this material being in our fabrics. I asked Dr. Smith if we needed to be concerned. He passed on the following information.

Formaldehyde is one of the leading industrial raw materials. It reacts with cotton, rayon, and other cellulose fibers to give them stability. Treated fibers will not wrinkle, crease, or shrink. Usually there is a trace of residual formaldehyde in newly manufactured fabrics, but it dissipates when it comes into contact with air. If there is a lot, it can give a sharp odor to the cloth, but this odor should not be confused with odors from other residual chemicals (starches and sizing) in the cloth.

A very critical test to detect this odor is to steam the cloth with a jet of steam from a tea kettle for fifteen seconds. A pungent burning odor indicates formaldehyde; other odors (e.g., fishy odors) do not indicate formaldehyde.

Formaldehyde is of almost no practical concern to U.S. consumers because most fabrics have so little of it. Those traces not already dissipated into the air are generally washed away in the first washing because formaldehyde is very water soluble. There was a time when stored fabrics could release enough formaldehyde to give an objectionable odor, but that was in the 1960s and those days are long gone. Because of federal regulations, any cloth made in the United States after 1980 will not have this problem.

Resin treatment is another stabilization method. Cotton fabric is saturated with resins, then cured to stabilize the fabric and reduce its tendency to distort. This treatment provides a slight crease resistance. Resin permanently sets the cotton cellulose structure in its cured shape/configuration.

FINISHING IMPERFECTIONS

There is always the possibility that imperfections will be created when fabrics are finished. The following list contains descriptions of the more commonly found imperfections in today's fabrics. These occur in the finishing, and are irreversible problems.

• *Bias skewed fabric:* When the filling (crosswise) yarns are straight but not at right angles to the warp (lengthwise) yarns. It is caused by improper alignment on the tenter frame. This is especially noticeable in plaids and stripes.

• **Bowed fabric:** When the filling yarns curve in the fabric and do not go straight across. It is also caused by improper tenter frame procedures, generally the result of too high a speed or machine misalignment. On-grain fabric will have less than $3/8$" variance in 45"-wide fabric.

• **Boardy fabric:** When the fabric is stiff, firm, and nondrapable compared to the standard for that fabric. It is caused by excessive amounts or improper application of chemical finishing agents.

• **Limp fabric:** When the fabric is too soft or without enough "body" compared to the standard for that fabric. It is caused by inadequate amounts or improper application of chemical finishing agents.

• **Tender goods:** Weakened fabric which results from excessive or improper application of chemical finishes or from aged (old) sulfur-dyed fabric.

• **Uneven finish:** When the fabric does not have the same character or amount of finish throughout the piece.

• **Mark-off:** A light mark that shows on the fabric when stroked or scraped with a hard object or fingernail. This is especially noticeable with pigment-dyed fabrics.

• **Mill flaws:** Defects caused in the weaving process such as slubs, broken ends, picks, misdraws, etc.

The final step the converter takes before the fabric leaves the plant is the *inspection*. Printing flaws, stains, spots, and weaving flaws are among the things the converter looks for when inspecting the cloth. When found, the fabric is marked for mending or repair, if possible. Mending is the actual repair of imperfections and the removal of major flaws caused by fabric construction processes. Often this will leave marks that give the fabric a "second quality" designation and it will be sold to discounters at a reduced rate.

Dyed and finished fabrics being inspected. This is where fabric is classified into first or second quality prior to shipment.

CHAPTER 8

LEARNING BY TESTING

In this chapter you will learn about your quilting fabrics and their care. I urge you to use this chapter as a workbook, actually perform the tests as you are reading through the chapter, and record your results. Once you see the results, you will see how important this information is to the health and well-being of your finished projects.

If you take the time to learn how to perform these tests and do them for each project, your fear and frustration with fabrics will end. I would ask that you do all this with an open mind to learning. You will love the comfort level your knowledge brings you.

"Why bother with all this?" you ask. The answer is: options. Until now quilters were told they had to prewash their fabrics to keep them from bleeding and shrinking. They were not instructed how to prewash them safely, just to wash them. When they saw bleeding, they automatically assumed the fabric had unstable dye, and that all the excess dye had to be washed out before they used the fabric. They never asked why the fabric bled—they just accepted the fact that it did.

Until now quilters were told they had to prewash their fabrics to keep them from bleeding and shrinking.

Quilters also felt that by prewashing they would reduce shrinkage. This is true, but what gives an antique quilt that wonderful crumply look that many of us love? Shrinkage. And if we want that look in some of our quilts, especially antique reproductions, we must get that shrinkage in the finished quilt.

We need to learn to make choices based on our own tastes and desires for our quilts. Sometimes you may choose to prewash and other times you may not. Just because it is common practice to prewash, and we have been told to do it for years, does not mean that it has to be done. I personally choose not to prewash my fabrics when making quilts, but I always test for the various types of colorfastness the fabrics may have to hold up to, depending on the way I am using the quilt. Even if I know I am going to prewash the fabric, I will still test it before prewashing to learn about the properties of the fabric I am working with. If I only prewash, and I see bleeding or migration, I won't know what really caused the fabric to misbehave unless I perform the tests beforehand. I could possibly damage the fabric unnecessarily by washing it in a manner that causes problems, whereas if I know the water is too high in chlorine, or the detergent is too strong for the dye, I can adjust what I am doing, still prewash the fabric, and have the color remain safe. Testing the fabric first helps you predict how it will behave in the finished quilt.

The following tests are easy and painless to perform. No special equipment is necessary; most of the items you will use you already have in the house. By doing each of the tests you will learn a lot about the fabrics you put into your quilts and save time, money, and disappointment knowing how your fabric will perform.

In order for you to get the most information from the test results, I encourage you to use the Fabric Analysis sheet found on page 75, or your own variation of it. The information provides not only a record for the next time you want to use that fabric, but also helps you identify trends among different fabrics and brands.

Some of the tests build upon the last, so keep the solutions in the jars until you know you will not need them.

This chapter includes many of the tests you can do to increase your options for handling fabrics—in general and for each individual project. With more information you will make better choices and achieve successful results with different styles and looks in your quilts.

In the following pages you will learn to test for fiber content, thread count, colorfastness to crocking, chlorine, alkali, detergents, color transference, and light fading, as well as shrinkage—a lot to learn, but fascinating once you start. Think of this as an adventure and have fun!

BURN TEST

The burn test is a good preliminary step for identifying the fabric you are testing. It can tell you whether you have a natural or synthetic fiber fabric.

1. Unravel one or two yarns from the warp, lengthwise direction, of your fabric. If you are testing batting (or any other nonwoven), snip a slender strip off the batt.
2. If possible, untwist the yarns so the fibers are in a loose mass. With batting use the fiber.

3. Hold the loosened fibers in a pair of tweezers and move them toward a flame from the side.
4. Observe the reaction as they approach the flame.

Cotton and flax are natural cellulosic fibers. Rayon and lyocel are manufactured regenerated cellulose fibers that will render the same results in a burn test. They do not shrink away as they approach the flame. They ignite on contact and burn quickly. When removed from the flame, they will continue to burn with an afterglow. They smell similar to burning paper and leave a light, feathery residue, light to charcoal gray in color.

Wool and silk are natural protein fibers and react differently. When they approach the flame, they curl away from it. Wool burns slowly, and silk will burn slowly and sputter. Wool is self-extinguishing, and usually silk is too. They both smell like burning hair. The residue of burned wool is a brittle, small black bead. Silk will also leave a black, crushable bead.

There are many synthetic fibers, but most commonly used with cotton, or as a cotton substitute, is polyester. When polyester fibers

Burn test used to identify types of fiber

A WORD OF CAUTION:
Use care when performing the tests described in this book. Make sure you have adequate space, a clean, flat surface, and have read and understand the directions before you begin.

approach a flame, they fuse, melt, and shrink away from the flame. In the flame they burn slowly and continue to melt. The melting fibers drip and have a chemical odor. They will self-extinguish when removed from the flame, but the residue left is a hard, tough, gray or tawny bead.

THREAD (YARN) COUNT

Thread count is another factor that quilters should take into consideration when purchasing fabrics for a quilt. As demand for cotton fabric grows, so does the supply of inferior print and solid fabrics. Because of this, we must learn to recognize high-quality fabric—and one consideration is the thread count. Today some of the finest quilting fabric is 68 x 68. This means that there are 68 threads per inch in both the warp and filling directions (before washing). There can easily be a slight variance due to faulty or casual processing, or by design. In this case we might say the thread count is 68 x 68 + or - 2. As you would expect, the thread count can go lower, for example, 60 x 60. This fabric tends to have a beefier hand because fatter yarn is used. The addition or omission of starches and finishes can also beef up the fabric. Remember that the same print can be printed on different qualities of greige goods for different markets and end uses. The selvage will show the same company name, designer name, etc., because the screens and rollers have that etched into them. This gets printed regardless of the construction, so do not use selvages as an indicator of quality. Muslin, which is essentially cleaned greige goods, also varies widely. There are numerous thread counts available, from 54 x 68 to 68 x 68, each appropriate for different end uses.

The issue of thread count affects quiltmaking more than is commonly thought. Thread count is one determinant of how many years a fabric can last, what chance the batting will have of coming through the fabric, what percentage of shrinkage there will be, and how high the print quality will be. Today's consumer who does not realize that thread count (and dye and finish quality) can fluctuate within a brand, within a season, and within different types of retailers, can be caught off guard. Thread count is not stated on the bolt board. Price can often be used as an indicator, but with today's discount stores and mass merchandisers, you cannot always depend on the price or the label to determine quality or consistency.

... you cannot always depend on the price or the label to determine quality or consistency.

Lower thread counts in today's cotton fabrics mean that all free fibers on the surface of polyester batting can migrate through the cloth, causing bearding. Bonded batts will not show bearding right away, but they too will eventually beard. The only way around this is to consider using cotton batts. One-hundred percent cotton batts break down into a powder, as the staple is too small to show on the surface. Lighter colored fabrics show this bearding problem less than darker fabrics, but it happens nonetheless. Polyester has the worst track record for bearding, and some wool batts are also susceptible to bearding. However, batting is not the only culprit; fabric weave can also cause bearding.

When you are learning to identify the quality of cloth, start to notice the feel, or the "hand" of a fabric. You will often find the softer and more supple the fabric, the higher the thread count. An example of this would be the difference in the feel between dress goods and decorator fabrics. (It must be noted here that with the new softer finishes, this can often be deceiving).

Take the time to count the threads in various fabrics and you will learn how to identify good quality. By comparing the thread count to the hand of the fabric, you will start to educate your eye and hand to what you are seeing and feeling and how it relates to performance.

THREAD (YARN) COUNT TEST

To count threads, you will need either a good strong magnifying glass, a photography loupe, or a pick glass, a sheet of four-to-the-inch graph paper, and a pin or other sharp pointed item.

If you are using a magnifying glass or loupe, cut a one-inch square from the center of a sheet of graph paper. This provides you with a window from which you will measure the fabric. Place the window anywhere on the fabric, aligning it to the yarns of the weave. You are

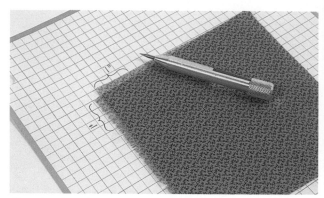
Counting threads from a frayed edge

looking for weaves with no holes or irregularities in them. Using your magnifying device and a pin or sharp point, actually count the threads in each direction.

A pick glass has a one-inch square built in on the base and is easy to use. Place the one-inch platform on the fabric and count the threads in the one-inch opening.

A very easy way to count threads is to count the threads at the edge of the cloth. Using four-to-the-inch graph paper and a two-inch square piece of fabric, unravel several threads from one corner, in both warp and fill directions. Place the square on the graph paper and count the thread in one grid of the graph paper. Multiply this by four to get the thread count

Tools used to determine thread count

for an inch. Repeat in the other direction, and in different locations, to eliminate the margin of error.

To review, a fabric that counts out to 68 x 68 or 66 x 66 will serve you very well, and is today considered a high-grade quilting fabric. Sheeting that counts out to 60 x 60 and is made from heavier yarns is also a good choice. Thin yarn weaves below 68 x 68 can be problem fabrics, but are readily available. Compare the wear and performance in your quilts of these low thread count fabrics with the higher thread count fabrics. If you have older quilts, compare the thread count with the amount of wear.

As you begin counting threads, you will be able to identify different types of weaves. Broadcloth, often referred to as a quilter's fabric, is a tightly woven, lustrous cotton or polyester/cotton blend fabric in a plain weave with a crosswise rib. It resembles poplin, but has a finer rib. The rib weave is a modification of the plain weave. It often has a different number of yarn plies and sizes in warp and fill directions. Yarns in one direction give the appearance of being heavier than yarns in the other direction. This results from having more warp yarns per inch than fill yarns and having these packed tightly together. When counting threads on broadcloth, anything higher than 96 x 54 is advisable. Since broadcloth allows fiber migration from batting and is difficult to press, its use in quiltmaking is not recommended.

COLORFASTNESS

Colorfastness refers to the permanence of color or its ability to remain unchanged throughout the useful life of the article to which it has been applied; to withstand use conditions, e.g., washing (washfastness); expo-

sure to light (lightfastness); and rubbing (crockfastness). No coloring agent used for textiles is absolutely fast to all conditions of use or environmental exposures. The degree of colorfastness is tested by standard procedures. Textile materials often must meet certain fastness specifications for a particular use. Exposure to water, washing agents, rubbing, sunlight, bleaches, atmospheric gases, and other factors usually produce color changes. A fabric's color stability should be tested before it is made into anything in order to determine if the fabric's performance will be satisfactory for the particular end use.

Exposure to water, washing agents, rubbing, sunlight, bleaches, atmospheric gases, and other factors usually produce color changes.

Many things relate to the colorfastness of a fabric: fiber type, type of dye used, dyeing or printing processes used, types of finishes applied to the fabric, as well as the action of laundering detergents, and temperature and chlorination of the water. Excessive heat in drying and even the residue of detergents not completely washed out of the material can cause color problems.

Testing labs have specialized equipment and highly trained technicians that perform over thirty tests to evaluate color changes. The changes that affect quiltmakers most readily are loss of color to light, washing, and abrasion. Each dye has different fastness properties. For example, compare the four most commonly used coloring agents in today's cotton fabrics.

NAPTHOL (AZOIC) DYES	
lightfastness	good
washfastness	excellent
crockfastness and chlorinefastness	good

Heavy (darker) shades tend to have poorer crockfastness.

SULFUR DYES	
lightfastness and washfastness	excellent
crockfastness	good
chlorinefastness	poor

Some sulfur dyes cause weakening of fabric if stored for great lengths of time.

FIBER REACTIVE DYES	
washfastness, and crockfastness	excellent
lightfastness	good
chlorinefastness	poor

PIGMENTS	
lightfastness	excellent
washfastness (hand)	fair
chlorinefastness	excellent

The differences between dyes and pigments need to be taken into consideration when choosing fabrics for specific end uses. A wall quilt exposed to light might not age well if the fabrics were dyed with Napthol dyes. A baby quilt will not look fresh and bright after several launderings if the fabric was dyed with fiber reactive or sulfur dyes and the water had excessive amounts of chlorine in it. However, by testing your fabrics before washing or using them you can avoid some of these potential problems. For example, if the fabric you test is not lightfast and it will be exposed to a lot of light, you know to find another fabric. If the fabric is losing color in the wash test, determine if it is the detergent or too much chlorine in the water, and try to correct the problem or select a different fabric. When you take the time and responsibility to test and learn about your fabrics, your quilts will reflect your knowledge and stay bright and healthy for a long time.

The following pages include several tests which have been adapted from standardized textile tests for you to test your fabrics at home.

Printed fabrics often will crock more easily than dyed fabrics because most of the coloring agent of printed fabric is on the surface and not inside the fiber as it is with dyed fabric.

Crocking

Crocking is the transference of color from rubbing one colored fabric against another. Dark shades are more likely to crock than light shades. This is because there is more colorant in and on the dark fabric, therefore more dye can be rubbed off. Printed fabrics often will crock more easily than dyed fabrics because most of the coloring agent of printed fabric is on the surface and not inside the fiber as it is with dyed fabric. The fabric will crock more easily when it is wet or damp because the moisture assists in removing dye.

Washing or dry cleaning may affect crocking test results. However, the test can be performed before and/or after laundering and the results will still be useful.

Loss of color from crocking on surface blocks and binding

DRY CROCKING TEST

You can test for crockfastness in the store before purchasing a fabric. Using a piece of dry white cotton cloth approximately four inches square, cover the end of your index finger. Hold the cloth on your finger and rub ten times forward and ten times back over an approximate-ly four-inch length of the colored fabric. Rub in the bias direction (diagonal). Use the same motion and pressure for each stroke. Examine the small rubbed area of the white cotton. You are looking for the amount of color that has rubbed off. If there is any color, it could be slight, noticeable, or pronounced. Repeat for each colored fabric you are testing.

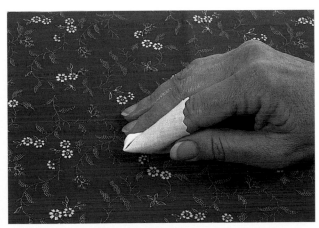

Wrap finger with white cloth and rub on surface of fabric.

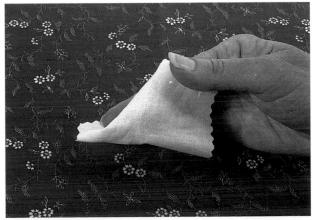

Check for color loss from crocking.

WET CROCKING TEST

You can also perform a wet (damp) crocking test on colored fabrics, using another four-inch square piece of the same white cotton cloth. This piece should be saturated with water and then squeezed out. Use the same procedure as for the dry test, but rub in a different area of the colored fabric. What are your results? Rate the same way as before.

For large prints with several colors, use a rotating motion for each color in the fabric. A lengthwise stroke could cross several colors, making it difficult to determine which color was crocking. Use the same white cloth, rotating on one color at a time. Once you are familiar with the testing process, practice it on scraps of fabrics you have used previously. If you know a fabric has had crocking problems, compare the crocking test results of this fabric with another fabric that did not have crocking problems. Gradually you will recognize the degree of rub-off that is acceptable and the degree that is not.

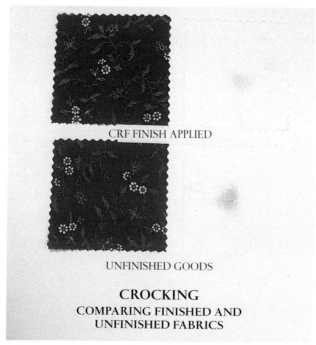

CRF FINISH APPLIED

UNFINISHED GOODS

CROCKING
COMPARING FINISHED AND UNFINISHED FABRICS

Finishes on fabrics can protect the fabric surface from severe crocking.

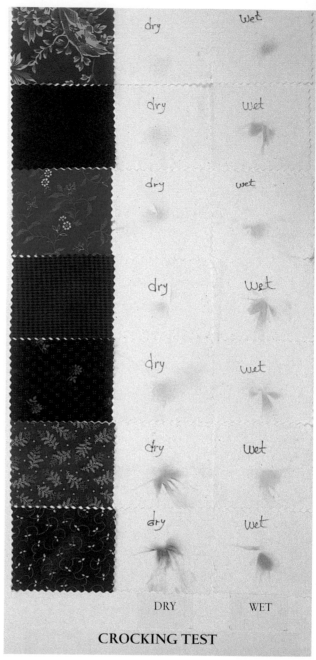

DRY   WET

CROCKING TEST

Varying degrees of color loss on a variety of fabrics from dry and wet testing

You will often find fabrics that lose color to the iron and adjoining fabric. These fabrics also leave the bed of the sewing machine colored, and your hands and ironing board stained. This indicates a crocking problem so be prepared for a frosted look on the surface of these fabrics as they age.

LIGHTFASTNESS

Lightfastness is the ability of a fabric to stand up to light. Dyed fabrics that are exposed to light can, in time, fade or change color. Both natural sunlight and artificial lights can cause damage to color. In general, light pastel colors fade more easily than dark ones, especially pinks and turquoises. But dark colors crock more than light ones.

The damage caused to a fabric from light depends on the intensity of the light source and the amount of exposure, as well as the properties of the dyestuff. Weather conditions, the season of the year, your relative height above sea level, and the distance you are from the equator will all affect sunlight intensity. Smoggy environments tend to filter and diffuse the light intensity more than clean, clear air. The proximity to artificial light sources also affects lightfastness. In general, the intensity of sunlight causes more serious lightfast damage than artificial light sources.

If you plan to make a wall quilt for a wall exposed to bright light, or a quilt for a bed in a room where light comes in from a window, it is advisable to first test your chosen fabrics for lightfastness.

Severe damage to the border fabric from exposure to light, but little fading shown on stripe in pieced blocks. Shows how dyes perform differently when exposed to the same light.

The standard method of testing for lightfastness in the home is the sunlight method. The samples need to be placed behind glass and exposed to sun from 9:00 a.m. to 3:00 p.m., at a minimum. All-day exposure is best, but sunlight intensity is most severe from 9:00 a.m. to 3:00 p.m. The samples should be placed where shadows from objects in the vicinity will not fall upon them. Repeat for approximately five summer days or eight winter days. Running the tests for consistent lengths of time allows you to make comparisons between a number of exposures.

Fabric that has been washed can react differently than unwashed fabric. I would suggest you run the following test using two sets of samples: one prewashed and one unwashed set. Compare the differences, if any.

Cut one 3" x 6" sample from each fabric you want to test. Attach the test pieces, one under the other, on a piece of posterboard large enough to accommodate the samples. Align the edges with each other. Cut another piece of cardboard 3" x the length of the samples, and position the pieces vertically on top of the column so that one-half of each swatch is covered. Staple this strip of cardboard to the top of the piece holding the swatches, creating a hinge. This allows half the sample to be exposed to the sun, and when the cardboard is lifted, a comparison can be made.

Tape the swatch holder to a window with the appropriate exposure. (You may need to move the sample during the day to keep constant exposure to sunshine). After exposure for three sunny days, examine the swatches for fading by raising the hinged cardboard. Each day thereafter, examine the exposure. Make a note of how many days or hours of exposure it

Preparing washed and non-washed samples for lightfastness test

A comparison of fading rates between different fabrics

takes to see noticeable fading. Some fabrics may take months of direct sunlight to produce noticeable fading, while others may show damage readily.

By placing the samples in direct sun for a minimum of six hours at a time, you have controlled the time element of the test. The actual fading can take much longer if the fabric is in a protected area of the house, with indirect, diffused light. If fading occurs on your samples, you know it is inevitable it will happen in your quilts, but you can be prepared for it. If the fabric is in a quilt on a bed or wall that gets six hours of sun a day, it is real life—not accelerated. It doesn't even take direct sunlight for serious fading to occur. There is no cure for fading, so carefully consider whether you want to use questionable fabric or not.

A standard for rating lightfastness has been developed by the lightfastness committee of the American Association of Textile Chemists and Colorists (AATCC). In the textile labs apparel fabrics are tested for a period of forty hours under accelerated conditions using high-intensity xenon or carbon arc lights. This is the equivalent of many months of exposure to sunlight. Pajama fabric is usually tested for only ten

hours (or not at all) because these fabrics' end use requires little resistance to sunlight. Drapery fabric, on the other hand, is tested for eighty hours, and canopy fabric for 160 hours. Automotive fabrics go up to 1,000 hours! Tests used for quiltmaking fabric are based on times set for apparel fabric.

When making quilts for the wall or bed, consider installing blinds or shades in the room so you can control the flow of light.

When making quilts for the wall or bed, consider installing blinds or shades in the room so you can control the flow of light. Consider keeping the blinds closed during the brightest part of the day. If the blinds are open, fold the quilt back on the bed so there is no light on the quilt surface. Quilts that are displayed throughout the home fare best when placed where there is minimal outside light exposure.

FROM FIBER TO FABRIC

WASHFASTNESS

I find the topic quiltmakers are most concerned about is how to wash their fabrics safely. A fabric's tendency to bleed or stain strikes concern and uneasiness in most of us, and the thought of spending many hours making a quilt just to have it ruined when we wash it is daunting.

What if I told you that you did not have to worry needlessly about this anymore—that you could make beautiful quilts that would retain their color for years and years without even prewashing the fabrics? Think of the time you would save washing, drying, and ironing all those yards of fabric. The only requirement would be to spend a few minutes testing water and detergents for their compatibility with your fabrics. Interested? Read on.

Colorfastness is a generic term used by many quilters to describe a fabric's ability to be washed without losing color. This is not completely accurate. The term to describe the washability of a fabric is **washfastness**. This takes into consideration factors such as water, detergent, and temperature.

Washfastness is the ability of a fabric to withstand the effects of laundering. Although washing fabric can result in the removal of dye, it is not inevitable. Most quiltmakers get quite upset when they see lost color in the wash water. However, this really tells them nothing about the fastness of the color. What needs to be determined is whether the color will stain another fabric, referred to as *color migration*. In color migration the dye in the water is redeposited onto other fabrics. Overall staining can even occur without a noticeable amount of dye from the original fabric in the water. Often dye that is deposited onto a fabric can be washed out with no permanent staining. If color in the water doesn't always stain the fabric, but some-

times can, or color staining occurs in fabrics when there is no color in the water, it can be very confusing. But like the old saying says, confusion is the dawn of knowledge. This is why we must test our fabrics *before* deciding to prewash or not.

When cotton fabrics are resin treated in the finishing process, they become extremely resistant to bleeding-off and staining. Quilters should always try to use resin-finished cotton goods. To detect whether resins are present, give the fabric a good shot of steam from the iron or teakettle and then smell the odor from the fabric. Most resin-treated fabrics will give off a mildly pungent odor.

As you can see, there are many variables affecting a fabric's washfastness. Chemistry is a powerful force that we need to understand before we make assumptions about how our fabrics will behave. For example:

- Did you know that the water temperature you wash your cottons in can affect their ability to retain their color? Have you heard that some people are taught to boil their fabrics to make sure that they are safe, when in reality this is exactly what damages the color?

- Did you know that the chlorine found in normal amounts in processed tap water can cause some dyes to release their color, but that you can control this problem?

- Did you know that detergents can be very damaging to the binders that hold the pigments onto the surface of the cloth and can be harmful to some fiber reactive dyes because of the chlorine content?

- Did you know that many fabrics do not lose their color in water, but when sewn to another fabric can transfer color at the seam?

- Did you know that prewashing fabrics will not necessarily render them washfast? There are many things we do after we prewash to cause stress, fading, or bleeding in our fabrics. We blame the fabrics—when we actually have the ability to prevent many of the problems.

This is why I so fervently believe that we must start learning more about textiles, colorants, and chemicals. Once we know what is causing the problems, we can take action to prevent them. I hope you enjoy the adventure.

Water Temperature

Let's begin by discussing water temperature. When I began lecturing about textiles several years ago, I said that baby bath (or tepid) water was the general guideline for washing cotton fabrics. Later I felt I needed to be more specific, so I talked to a textile chemist about this. He said that cold water was best for washing cottons. When I asked *how* cold, his answer was: "You know, turn-on-the-faucet cold." But I *didn't* really know, because at the time I was in South Carolina. There, if I turned on the faucet to get cold water, it would be pretty warm compared to tap water at home in Colorado. I realized "cold" tap water depended on where you were and what time of year it was. In the south the water is not much colder in the winter than in the summer, but in the Rockies and northern areas the cold water from the faucet in the winter can make your hands ache. And in some areas the water in the winter is so cold the detergent won't dissolve to activate the sanitization. Therefore, it is worthwhile to have some standard of what is considered "cold" water.

According to the AATCC, wash water temperatures are as follows:

Very cold	60°	+ or - 5°F
Cold	80°	+ or - 5°F
Warm	105°	+ or - 5°F
Hot	120°	+ or - 5°F
Very hot	140°	+ or - 5°F

I have found through much testing that water temperatures between 80° and 85°F give me very good results. Any warmer, and faint color often appears in the water.

To test water temperature for yourself, place the same richly dyed dark fabric in jars with different water temperatures and note how warm the water is when color starts to appear in the water. If you take the time to repeat this for different fabrics, you will start to see a pattern of what temperatures are safe.

Chlorinefastness

The next factor to consider is the level of chlorine in the water. Many of the color loss problems we see in fabrics are due to their lack of fastness to chlorine. Fiber reactive dyes often used in quiltmaking cottons are especially sensitive to chlorine but other dyes can also react. These fabrics, which are generally the rich, jewel-tone colors, will often bleed into water that has excessive chlorine in it. Are you surprised to find that the fabric may not be the problem, but the water itself?

Have you ever turned on the faucet and the tap water smelled like chlorine? Perhaps this is the state of your water all the time. If you fill the washing machine and the water smells like a swimming pool—look out!

A normal level of chlorine in drinking water is three parts per million (ppm) if well controlled, but often the city puts in excess amounts depending on various conditions. You can usually smell it if it is over 3 ppm. Even

3 ppm can cause problems for some fabrics. It is suspected the safe level for fabrics is less than 0.1 ppm.

CHLORINE TEST

So how do you know if chlorine is a problem with your water? Begin by filling a pint jar with cold tap water (see temperature chart on page 64). Place a sample of fabric in the water. Use dark, rich, jewel-tone colors such as reds, cranberries, purples, rusts, etc. Do this with several different fabrics. Many of the fabrics which are dyed and printed with fiber reactive dyes are very sensitive to chlorine. If you do not see color in the water when you test several different fabrics, then you probably do not have a chlorine problem. Color loss is not the only culprit, however. Color change can also occur.

Test rich, dark colors in your tap water to detect sensitivity to chlorine.

If you do see color, follow the next step. Fill another jar with distilled or purified water. Place another piece of the same fabric in the second jar, making sure the water temperature is the same in both jars. If there is color in the tap water, but not in the purified water, you can assume that the chlorine in your water is causing some of the color loss. (If there is color loss in the purified water, it is likely the fabric is not fast to water in general and could possibly be a problem no matter what you do.)

To verify that the fabric is sensitive to chlorine, put a very small amount of chlorine bleach in the purified water and put the fabric into it. If you immediately lose some color, you will need to neutralize the water so it does not continue to affect your fabric. The effects of chlorine depend on several different factors. The reaction rate of sodium hypochlorite (chlorine) bleach on fabric or dye is very sensitive to time, temperature, concentration, and pH (if made unstable with acids).

Neutralizing Chlorine

Two of the chemicals available to neutralize the chlorine in your water are sodium bisulfite and sodium thiosulfate. Both are known as antichlor. This chemical, when added to the wash and rinse water, will eliminate the chlorine problem. Use one gram per liter to de-chlorinate test water, and about three ounces (or the amount recommended by the manufacturer) to de-chlorinate a washing machine load. **NOTE: Be sure you understand and follow all manufacturers' safety recommendations for the use of their products.**

In the chlorine test, whether you lose color or the color changes, you will need to neutralize the water so it does not continue to affect your fabric.

Sodium bisulfite is a preservative used in some restaurants for the lettuce in their salad bars and is available from restaurant supply businesses. Other products to neutralize chlorine for fish tanks (from pet stores) and swimming pools (from swimming pool and spa supply stores) are also readily available. Follow instructions on the individual containers.

To see how sodium bisulfite works: Fill the washing machine with water. Add one fluid ounce of bleach. Wash one half of a piece of fiber-reactive dyed fabric in the water. (Try brilliant red or green cotton knits. Knits are often dyed with fiber reactive dyes.) Repeat the test, but after adding the bleach and before adding the other half of the fabric, put 80 grams (3 ounces) of sodium bisulfite in the water. Wash. Compare the two different samples for fading. You will see how damaging chlorine can be to some dyes, and how sodium bisulfite can help eliminate the problem.

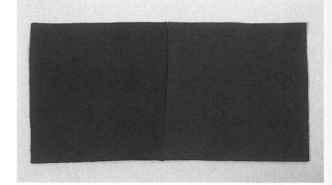

Progressive color loss from continual exposure to chlorine in water

Jar on the left shows chlorine damage. Jar on the right contains water treated with sodium bisulfite and demonstrates how the same fabric reacts.

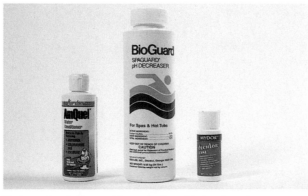

Various chemicals used to neutralize chlorine in water

Laundering Fabrics: Detergents and Soaps

Consumers tend to get confused about soaps and detergents, water hardness, and how they affect cleaning. Knowledge of cleaning processes is useful to prevent damage to your fabrics.

Water hardness is the total concentration of calcium and magnesium ions, also known as calcium carbonate equivalent, measured in terms of parts per million of hardness. Water hardness ranges from soft to very hard. A higher degree of hardness will adversely affect the sudsing and cleaning action of the cleanser. Greater amounts of suds are produced when water softeners are added. However, the amount of suds is not an indication of cleaning action. Sudsing agents are added to detergents only to satisfy consumers. Suds do not relate to cleaning. In some areas the water contains only 30 parts per million (ppm) of hardness. In these areas, soap works fine. If hardness is over 300 ppm, soap can cause problems. To find out about the water in your area, call the local water department.

There are two types of cleansers used for home laundry: detergents and soaps. Soaps are metallic salts of a fatty acid. Detergents are organic compositions (other than soap), produced by chemical synthesis. Both of these products lower the surface tension so fabrics absorb wetness more easily. They also hold soil in suspension so it does not settle back onto the fabric. Soap is affected by hardness. Detergent is generally not.

Commercial cleaning products are formulated to contain water softeners, brighteners to improve whiteness, and agents that do not let soil redeposit on the fabric surface. Some contain bleaches. They do not form curd in hard water. No special treatments for water are required for their use unless the water is very hard.

Some detergents contain high concentrations of phosphates. These are effective in most types of water. Phosphates reduce the water hardness by attaching themselves chiefly to the calcium and magnesium salts in the water. They will work themselves into natural water resources, causing environmental imbalances. Because of this ecological concern, many local and state governments have outlawed their use.

Soaps are excellent cleansers in soft water, but in hard water (over 300 ppm), they combine with minerals to form an insoluble curd which is difficult to rinse out. A mechanical water softener is required for effective use of soaps.

Neither soaps nor detergents themselves adversely affect textile fibers. They can, however, adversely affect finishes and cause certain dyes to run.

Excessive or insufficient use of soaps and detergents is a major problem in home laundry. Too little cleanser causes soil redeposition. Excessive amounts are difficult to rinse out and remove, causing harshness to the fabric, and can also cause soil redeposition. Cleansers that are not totally rinsed out may also cause skin rashes and breathing sensitivity. Overloading the washer does not allow an adequate amount of water to thoroughly rinse the cloth.

A general guideline for choosing a detergent is to look for a product with the least amount of ingredients. The more ingredients, the harsher the product tends to be. The best cleaning agents are non-ionic and anionic detergents. Look for clear (hand dishwashing) liquid products that say "non-ionic surfactant" on the label. One example is Ultra Ivory® dishwashing liquid. Non-ionic types are most effective at low temperatures.

A product that is now getting a lot of attention from quiltmakers is sodium lauryl sulfate, also known as Orvus Paste®. This is a synthetic detergent designed to duplicate the soapmaking ingredient in coconut oil—lauric acid. As a synthetic, it eliminates the tendency of coconut oil-based soaps to form the curd, and it retains its cleaning power, even in the processed, acid-type water found in many of today's cities. Its relatively high viscosity also helps it handle greasy soil. This product leaves both dyed colors and the "hand" of the fabric unchanged. It has a neutral pH and is especially safe with the fiber-reactive dyes used in many of our cotton fabrics and threads.

Orvus Paste is readily available at feed and pet supply stores. It is considered a horse shampoo and is very safe for use on animals and humans. The product rinses out completely, so fewer rinsings of a quilt are necessary. It is also safe enough to bathe in, which is a criterion I use for caring for natural fibers of any kind. The main cleaning agent is found in most hair shampoos.

Most manufacturers of soaps or detergents do not sell pure products. They dilute them with various materials. This makes them easier to handle and use. But, because each is different, you must use the recommended amount, which varies from product to product. For example, if you use Ultra Ivory, ¼–⅓ cup in a washer is plenty. If you see suds in the final rinse water—you used too much. If you use Orvus, 1–2 tablespoons per washload is usually sufficient.

Testing for Washfastness

What you will learn by testing fabrics for washfastness is how a detergent can affect a dye in the water. At first, I recommend that you test several detergents so you can see different results on the same fabric. Once you have become comfortable with a detergent that performs safely in your water, you should then only need to test fabrics with that one detergent. The major consideration for this is that quilts made from fabrics tested in one particular detergent be laundered only in that detergent in the future. The use of quilt care labels can help you and future owners of your quilts protect the colors in the fabrics for many years.

Equipment used to test for washfastness

To learn the process of color testing your fabrics, start with five pint jars. Save the solution results in each jar for subsequent tests. Record your results using the Fabric Analysis sheet on page 75 and keep the solution in the jars. Fill each jar ¾ full with tepid water.

Note: Before color testing, run a chlorine test if you suspect there is a problem. Remember, the temperature of water safest for cotton fabrics is 80°-85°F. No extremes. Hot water can destroy the finish on fabrics. Wash and rinse in tepid water for the safest results. This applies to all natural fibers.

Next, dissolve one teaspoon of each detergent in a different jar. Use a variety of detergents, such as Ultra Ivory dishwashing liquid, Orvus Paste, normal laundry detergents such as Tide®, Arm & Hammer® or Shaklee®, and any other heavy-duty all-purpose detergent if desired, baby shampoo, and any others. Choose at least five different products.

Select a fabric color you feel will be a problem—such as red, rust, or dark green. Cut the fabric into 4" or 5" squares—one for each jar. Add the sample to the jar and shake frequently to simulate a washing action. Allow the fabric to remain in the solution for up to ten minutes.

Remove the samples and keep the jars in order. Examine the washing solution for color loss. Rinse the samples at least twice in another jar and look for any color loss in this water during rinsing. Dry the sample, and compare it with the original fabric to determine whether any color change has occurred. If there is no evidence of color loss in any of these steps, the fabric is washfast (colorfast to washing) in that detergent. The surprising thing that happens during this test is that the same fabric can lose color in one detergent but not another.

ALKALI TEST

Bleeding is often caused by alkali in the soap or detergent. You can test this by treating the water with bicarbonate solution, soda ash (baking powder), or ammonia. Alkali promotes bleeding of many dyes (such as direct dyes); therefore this is a very important test of the fabric's washability in detergent.

Add to one cup of water 1 tsp. baking soda + 2 tsp. fresh household ammonia. Mix thoroughly. Heat to 150°F in a microwave or on a stove. Place a 5" square of cotton fabric into the solution. Stir for fifteen minutes. If this does not make the fabric bleed, you can be reasonably sure the fabric will be very resistant to normal washing.

I asked Dr. Brent Smith, who helped me with these tests, how much bleeding was too much. He responded by advising that we take several fabrics that are known to be good and several fabrics that are known to be bad. Then run the test on each to get a frame of reference. This goes for all the tests in this chapter. With a little experience, you can easily learn to recognize which fabrics will be a problem. Try it. You won't learn any other way.

Chemicals in detergents can also cause problems for a dye that would normally not have a problem. If you see color in the water, and wash and rinse the fabric until the water runs clear, you may have damaged the color needlessly. By taking the time to do this detergent test, you will see that if you have some jars with color in them, and some jars without color, it is an indication a chemical reaction between the water, fabric dye, and detergent is occuring. Therefore, you can safely assume that if you always wash that fabric in the safe detergent, you will not have dye stability problems with that fabric.

At this point you can decide whether to use the fabric unwashed—on the condition that a care label is added to the quilt stating which detergent to wash in. It is advisable to give a bottle of this detergent with the quilt—with full washing instructions—when giving it as a gift. If detergents are switched, bleeding can/will occur.

What if you have color in all the jars? Do you assume the fabric will always be a problem? Not necessarily. It is likely there is excess dye on the surface of the fabric and it is sloughing off into the water. But will it migrate onto another fabric and stain it? Is it happening because the fabrics have not been resin treated? Is there too much chlorine in the water?

Be sure to test your water for chlorine and your fabrics for resins if you have not already done so. You can also see that if you skip any of the steps, you don't have the whole picture, or the ability to know what is causing the problem.

COLOR MIGRATION TEST

The next step of the test is to determine whether color migration will be a problem. Cut 4" squares of the lightest fabric to be used in the project. Place a light fabric square and a square of the fabric in question in each jar of stained water. Shake them often over a period of ten minutes. Remove the samples and wring them out. Smooth them and compare to a dry sample of the same cloth. Have the light-colored samples picked up any color from the colored water? If the light fabrics are stained, the dye has migrated and can cause serious permanent problems in your quilt. If there is no color transfer, the dark fabric will bleed, but not migrate. You will find that these results can be different with each detergent tested.

Testing dark colors in water with various detergents

Bleeding is the loss of color when a fabric is immersed in water, a solvent, or similar liquid medium, and is a result of improper dyeing or the use of poor-quality dyes. Fabrics that bleed can stain fabrics (especially white and light shades) that are in contact with them when wet, but do not always cause staining. *Migration* is the actual movement of dye from one area of dyed fabric to another. This includes movement of color from the dyed area to the undyed area of the fabric and movement of color from one fabric to other fabrics in the same wash water. Although a label may state that the fabric is colorfast, it may not be colorfast to laundering (detergents). Fabrics may lose color, or bleed, without giving visible evidence of color change in the item itself. This occurs when excess dye has remained in the fabric. Other fabrics may bleed and migrate until all the excess dye is washed out completely, and then be safe. By then, however, more often than not, the color of the fabric has changed noticeably.

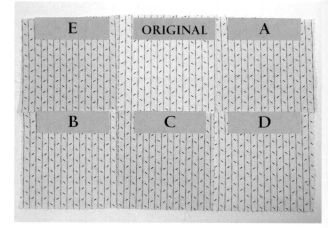

Comparing results of color migration from different detergents against the original cloth

COLOR TRANSFER TEST

Another problem quilters encounter when washing their quilts is referred to as *color transference*. This happens when wet fabrics are in contact with each other and two different colors touch. This next test is a wet color transfer test. Put two or more wet samples together, color/light/color/light, etc. (sandwich style), between two pieces of glass. Put a weight (jar of peanut butter or sixteen-ounce soup can) on top of the glass. Let them dry together overnight. Separate them and check for staining of the light fabrics. If this occurs, even though the fabric passed the other tests, you will know the quilt could be damaged by this problem. (Direct dyes seem to be the biggest offenders in color transference problems.)

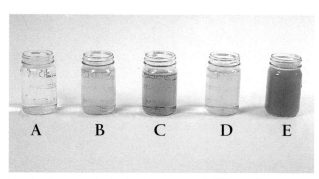

Varying degrees of color loss in water with different detergents

Testing light fabrics in stained water for color migration

Pressing wet dark and light fabrics between glass to test for color transference

FROM FIBER TO FABRIC

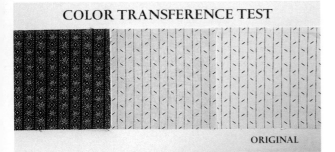

COLOR TRANSFERENCE TEST

ORIGINAL

Results of color transference test

Now you can make your choice of whether to prewash your fabric or not based on what you have witnessed. If the fabric in question passed all the tests, you can prewash the fabric safely because you know how to treat the water if needed, the temperature the water should be, and what detergent is safe for the fabric. You can also decide *not* to prewash, and rest assured you will not have problems as long as you repeat the things you learned in the testing process. If you see that your water and detergent combinations are safe and do not cause a problem with the dye stability of your fabrics, you can then decide whether to prewash or not based on the desired look you want for the finished quilt, the desired amount of shrinkage or the softness of hand, or allergies to unwashed fabrics.

Dry Cleaning

Often quilters will ask if dry cleaning is safe for cottons. I have talked to several dry cleaners and they prefer to see cottons washed in water as opposed to dry cleaning solvent. You can test for colorfastness to dry cleaning by immersing a 2" x 4" sample into cleaning solvent or spot cleaner for ten to twenty minutes. Check to see whether any color has bled into the cleaning solution. Then dry, and compare the sample with an original piece of fabric to determine if color change has occurred or if any bleeding represents excess dye only. A good guideline is to clean cotton in water.

SHRINKAGE

In Chapter 7 we discussed the different types of shrinkage. As mentioned, the most common problem relating to shrinkage is dryers. Drying at high temperatures is damaging to fabrics. You should test the temperature of your dryer using the methods covered in Chapter 7. AATCC gives the following tumble dry exhaust temperature parameters:

Normal or permanent press   144°-164°F
Delicate or synthetic   144°F

It might also be a good idea to remove the fabric or cotton products from the dryer when they are still slightly damp. Most shrinkage occurs during overdrying from 25% to 0% moisture. Air and line drying are two ways to avoid possible problems the dryer might cause, but air and line drying is slower, which gives more time for wet color transfer.

When you test for colorfastness, compare the shrinkage rates on the samples used. You will start to become more aware of how fabric behaves in different situations.

Concern about the amount of shrinkage in a fabric is often the reason quiltmakers prefer to prewash their fabrics. However, I suggest you test the fabrics first to determine if they truly have a damaging shrinkage rate, or if the tumble dryer is causing the shrinkage.

SHRINKAGE TEST

To test for shrinkage, cut a 22" square on the grain of the sample fabric. Two inches from the edges of the cloth, make marks two inches long, as shown in the following photo. Use a permanent marker or stapler.

For warp shrinkage, measure from A to B and C to D, before and after washing. For filling shrinkage, measure from A1 to C1 and B1 to

D1, before and after washing. By using the formula below, simple mathematical calculations will show percentage of shrinkage or stretch:

$$\% \text{ shrinkage (or growth)} = \frac{\text{Original length - New length}}{\text{Original length}} \times 100$$

If the new length is greater than the original length, then the calculated percentage is growth. If the original length is greater than the new length, the percentage is shrinkage.

Example

The shrinkage marks put both lengthwise and widthwise on the sample before washing were 18" apart. After washing, the marks placed lengthwise are 17.5" apart and the marks placed widthwise are 18.5" apart. Calculate the percentage of shrinkage or growth for each direction.

Length: $\frac{18 - 17.5}{18} \times 100 = 2.7\%$ shrinkage
(A-B, C-D)

Width: $\frac{18 - 18.5}{18} \times 100 = 2.7\%$ growth
(A1-C1, B1-D1)   (disregard the calculated minus (-) sign).

Overall shrinkage in one yard would be:
Fabric Width:

45" x 1.027 (growth) = 46.215 (or a little over 1" growth)

Fabric Length:

36" (one yard) x .027 (shrinkage) = 0.927 (or a little less than 1"/yd)

Shrinkage varies with fabric, but typical cotton fabric shrinkage is:

	L x W Knit	L x W Woven
Good	4% x 4%	2% x 2%
Fair	7% x 7%	4% x 4%
Poor	10% x 10%	6% x 6%

Compare samples that have been line or flat dried with those that have been tumble dried (after dryer temperature has been checked).

If only small pieces of fabric are available for testing, trim a 4" x 5" sample so the cut edges are parallel to warp and filling yarns. Clearly mark the warp and the filling directions. Try to cut the sample so the 5" side is the warp. Stitch the edges to prevent raveling. Place the sample on paper and draw around it so there is an outline of the original sample size.

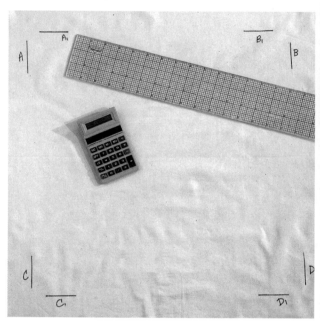

Testing for shrinkage

Testing for shrinkage using small samples

Using a pint jar and lid, wash the sample by hand, in the water temperature and detergent that will be used on the finished project. Rinse the sample thoroughly, dry, and press. Compare with the original size. Remember that if raveling does occur, the results will be misleading.

If you are looking at the shrinkage of a small piece, think about how a quilt is made. We sew many small pieces together and then quilt through two more layers. Each small piece of fabric shrinks very little, and when pieced with many others and secured by quilting to the batting and backing, the shrinkage of that one small piece of fabric is not significant. Therefore, since many fabrics shrink differently, one fabric alone will not likely affect the final look of the quilt.

Shrinkage of the batting and backing are more likely to affect the overall look of the quilt. Essentially one-piece units, they determine how much shrinkage will occur in the quilt based on fiber content of the batting, whether the backing has been prewashed or not, and how closely the layers are quilted together. Slight puckering might result if pieces shrink differently, but I have not seen this as a noticeable problem in the finished, washed quilt.

It should also be noted that seams tend to stabilize cloth. Fabric that is pieced and then quilted will shrink much less than the same size piece of fabric washed as a whole piece. There can be up to a 2% difference in shrinkage between the loose cloth and the stabilized (stitched) cloth.

I ran a test once to prove this to myself. I made two identical small quilt tops from fabric I had not prewashed. I quilted one and not the other. Then I washed both of them. The quilted top showed no signs of uneven shrinkage, just the overall look that the batting gave the quilt. The different fabrics in the unquilted top, on the other hand, did shrink unevenly.

Companies do not provide a lot of technical information about the fabrics we purchase. Up to now, consumers have not shown much interest. However, this is changing, and consumers are now demanding more information about the products they purchase. Care labeling has, to some extent, compensated for the absence of such information. While these labels are written to assure consumers that if given the care stated on the label, the product will not result in changes that cause product failure, care label regulations apply to apparel only. Any attempt to write care instructions for fabrics has been a voluntary act by a mill. Not knowing how the fabric will be used, the mill's technical staff prepare overly cautious recommendations. Below is a listing of "care" instructions given on the ends of bolts from six major companies printing fabrics for quiltmaking:

- Machine wash warm
- Normal cycle
- Tumble dry low or line dry
- Remove promptly
- Warm iron
- Do not dry clean
- Use non-chlorine bleach

It is advisable, when making a time consuming and valuable item like a quilt, that we slow down and take the time to completely test the fabrics for colorfastness to crocking, light, and washing. Once these tests are performed, you can then make intelligent, well-informed decisions as to whether to use the fabric at all, or if you prefer to prewash your fabric before using, or use it unwashed, just as you purchased it. The decision is yours.

SUMMARY

Above and beyond all this testing and investigating, I would like you to consider all the fabric we purchase and how we store it.

Let me challenge you to rethink your buying habits. I would suggest that you purchase ⅛–¼ yard lengths of the fabrics you are considering for a quilt. Take them home and test them. If the cloth passes all tests to your satisfaction, purchase the yardage needed. This way you aren't buying yards and yards of fabric only to find out it fails the tests. You will know that you are getting good quality and that the quilt will benefit from this for years to come.

If the fabrics you test "fail," advise your store and give them feedback. This will help the quilt shops avoid buying goods from vendors that repeatedly sell "failing" fabric. Once you start to monitor different brand names and note the results of the tests by brand, you will start to see a pattern. If these vendors continue to sell a lesser quality than they claim, we will have the knowledge to avoid purchasing from them. They want our business, and chances are the quality will come up once we start to gain knowledge.

One personal consideration for not prewashing before knowing what you are going to do with the fabric is the health of the fabric while in storage. Many of the cotton fabrics are finished with a mildew retardant. If the mildew retardant is washed out, depending upon your geographical location, mildew could get into your entire fabric collection. Finishes also help retard light damage, and when washed out, fading can be a potential problem for the fabrics in storage.

As a collection, unwashed fabric is more valuable to another fabric collector. Fabrics, as well as quilts, that have never been washed bring the highest prices at auction.

Furthermore, future quilts can be affected by automatically taking the fabric home and prewashing it. As you learn more about fabrics and battings, you will find that you may want to have options available to you when you are planning a quilt. Let's say that you want to make a 1930s reproduction, and you want the true look of an old quilt. This is achieved by allowing the fabric and batting to shrink together, giving the "puckers" so characteristic of older quilts. When you go through your fabric stash, you find that all your fabrics have been preshrunk. This is not going to help you achieve the look you want, and you will probably wind up purchasing new fabric for the project.

On the other hand, let's say that all your fabric is stored new, as you bought it. You decide to use a piece from some yardage you have, and use it unwashed. After testing for colorfastness, you make that quilt and still have what remains of the original piece. If for the next quilt you want to use that fabric and it needs to be prewashed for whatever reason, you only wash the amount you need for that current project. Then the next time you want to use the remaining fabric, it is still unwashed. See the pattern? You now have options available to you as never before. With each quilt you can determine how the fabric should be handled. You accommodate for each quilt, but retain the option for next time with the remaining fabric. Your fabric stash becomes a working tool.

I hope that through testing and observing the results you gain a real understanding of what is happening to the fabrics today, and what our responsibility to them is. With this comes a true comfort level when purchasing and using fabrics for quiltmaking.

FABRIC ANALYSIS

```
┌─────────────────────────┐
│                         │
│                         │
│                         │
│   Place fabric swatch here  │
│                         │
│                         │
│                         │
└─────────────────────────┘
```

Fabric Brand _____

(line name, number, style, etc.)

Dyed or Printed _____

Fiber Content _____

Thread Count _____ length (warp)

_____ width (filling)

1. Crockfastness Test (Use gray scale to evaluate color change.)

Dry Test _____   Wet Test _____

2. Lightfastness Test (Use gray scale to evaluate color change.)

Total number of hours tested _____ winter/summer

(circle one)

	Prewashed	Nonwashed
Day 3	_____	_____
Day 4	_____	_____
Day 5	_____	_____
Day 6	_____	_____
Day 7	_____	_____
Day 8	_____	_____

Gray Scale

75%   Pronounced

60%

45%   Noticeable

30%

15%   Slight

3. Washfastness Tests

Water Temperature _____

Presence of Chlorine   yes _____   no _____

Product used to neutralize chlorine: _____

Was an alkali test performed?   yes _____   no _____

Detergents (Use gray scale to evaluate color change).	A	B	C	D	E
% Color loss in water with detergents					
% Color migration onto light color fabric					
% Color transference by contact and pressure					

4. Dimensional Stability Test

Size of fabric tested _____ x _____

Temperature of wash water _____

Drying method   line _____   dryer _____   iron _____

Distance between marks before washing   length _____   width _____

Distance between marks after washing   length _____   width _____

5. Calculation of Shrinkage (Refer to page 72)

Original Length: _____ - Final Length: _____ ÷ Original Length _____ x 100 = % Shrinkage or Growth _____

Original Width: _____ - Final Width: _____ ÷ Original Width _____ x 100 = % Shrinkage or Growth _____

Overall size loss (or gain)   length _____   width _____

(See photocopy permission on page 2).

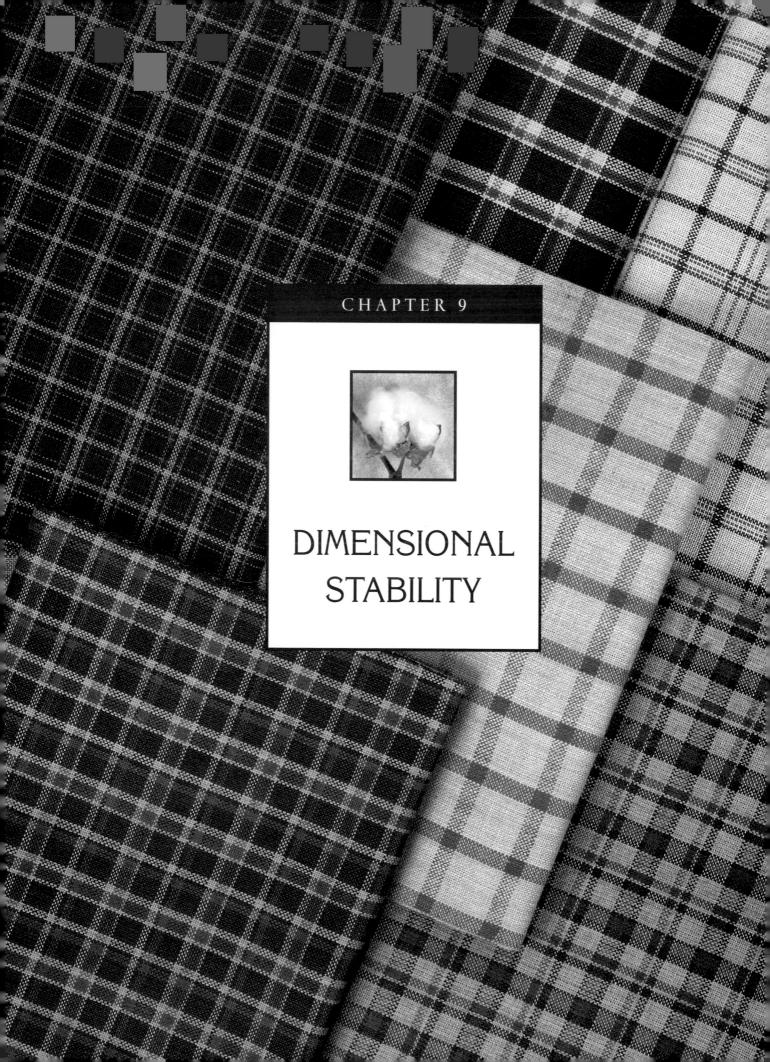

CHAPTER 9

DIMENSIONAL STABILITY

FABRIC GRAIN

Does fabric grain really make a difference in the outcome of your projects? Is grain placement important to a finished quilt? When and why should it be considered? Understanding fabric grain will help you decide how much importance you need to place on grainline for each project.

To review, woven fabrics are made by interlacing two sets of yarns at right angles to each other, the lengthwise yarns (warp yarns) and the crosswise (widthwise) yarns (filling yarns). The selvage runs along the lengthwise edge on both sides of the fabric. It is usually from ¼ to ½ inch wide and is actually a self edge. Its purpose is to ensure that the edge of the fabric will not tear when the cloth undergoes the stresses and strains of the finishing process.

Fabric grain is the lengthwise and crosswise yarns that are woven into fabric. When the grain is parallel to either the warp or filling yarns the fabric is said to be "on-grain." Lengthwise grain, which runs parallel to the selvage, has very little stretch. Crosswise grain, which runs perpendicular to the selvage, has more stretch. The most stretch is in the bias direction, or 45° to both sets of yarns. This is because the yarns bend and shift from the pulling force being exerted.

GRAIN STABILITY TEST

Fabric that is on-grain drapes and sews well. Fabric that is off-grain does not drape properly and stretches when you sew it. This is because the yarns are not at right angles to each other. To check the grain on a bolt of fabric, make sure the warp yarn that runs along the length of the fold does not have more than a ³⁄₈" variance. Crosswise grain can be checked by tearing the fabric across the width from selvage to selvage. The tear should align with itself, and be perpendicular to the selvages. Fabrics with more than a ³⁄₈" variance in 45"-wide fabric should be avoided; they will be very difficult to straighten and work with.

PRINT DISTORTION TEST

When checking the grain on the bolt, notice how the print aligns with the grain. You can tell if the print has been printed straight by examining the torn edge. A seemingly random print may be directional. The print actually takes on a diagonal stripe effect. If it is printed off-grain, you need to consider how you are using the fabric and whether this will affect the finished quilt. Too often you don't notice this problem until the quilt is finished and hung, and the off-grain fabric wavers.

Fabrics that are printed off-grain

Common dilemma for quilters. The fabric used in the border is printed *off-grain*, but needs to be cut *on-grain* to achieve borders that are flat and straight.

Many people do not consider the problem of grain and print distortion when they are piecing a quilt with many small pieces, since the pieces are often too small to straighten. However, you must still decide whether you can work around a definite print that runs off-grain. If the pieces are relatively small and that is most appealing for the design, then the pieces can be cut in alignment with the print. But if the piece in question is on a border, and straight grain is important to how well that quilt hangs or lays, the fabric should be cut with the grain. If the print is so off-grain that it detracts from the design of the quilt, it might come down to finding an alternative fabric. Print distortion can cause severe problems with plain blocks in a quilt top, sashings, borders, and backings.

Grain Direction

Grain direction can have a dramatic effect on color. Sateens and polished cottons show obvious color changes when turned in different directions. Prints with directional designs can also appear different when turned. Once you are aware of these types of fabrics, you can use this information to your advantage for special effects in some quilts. The Amish, who used a lot of sateen in their quilts, placed their pieces

in different directions on the quilt top and achieved the look of many different shades of one color. You can readily spot black sateen being used this way in Amish quilts. Any fabric with a sheen or nap will show noticeable color changes depending on placement direction. If you do not want or need to take advantage of this aspect in certain fabrics, be sure that all identical shapes have the same grain placement in order to appear the same.

Color change created by light reflecting off different grain directions of sateen

CUTTING VERSUS TEARING FABRIC

Although sometimes a fabric is off-grain, other times it is simply wrapped onto the bolt crooked. Many of these fabrics, however, can be straightened and put back on-grain, which brings me to the subject of tearing versus cutting fabric from the bolt. As with any issue, there are opinions on both sides—and both those who tear and those who cut fabric think they are right. I will outline the concerns and then share my thoughts on the matter.

If a fabric is cut at a perfect 90° angle to the selvage, you might think you have the exact amount of fabric you need. You must, however, consider whether the fabric is on-grain crosswise. You will need to look very closely to see how the filling yarns align with the warp yarns. Are they perfectly straight and even with the cut, or running off the cut edge at an angle? If they are not perfectly straight and even, you will need to straighten the fabric to get straight grain strips and pieces. To find the crosswise grain, tear a strip from the end of the fabric, on both sides. This can often add up to a large loss if the fabric is really off-grain. Once torn and straightened, you may find yourself short of the yardage needed for the project. If you detect this at the store, you will need to purchase up to ¼ yard extra just for straightening.

On the other hand, if the fabric is torn from the bolt, you automatically know if the fabric is on-grain or not. You will have exactly the same usable length on each selvage edge, even though the ends do not line up. The biggest argument against tearing is the streaking that occurs when darker printed colors are torn. When tearing, some of the threads will turn over, exposing the back side that has not been saturated or printed with dye. This damaged area is generally added to the yardage you are buying, at each end. Therefore, after straightening, this damaged area can be cut away, leaving you the exact yardage you purchased and needed for the project.

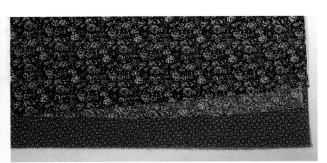

Tearing a piece of fabric crosswise will show if the fabric is printed on-grain, is bowed or skewed, is on the bolt straight, or if the grain has been misaligned when doubled and rolled onto the bolt.

Many people believe that by pulling the fabric bias in the opposite direction it is off, they can straighten the fabric.

If you find the torn edges of the fabric on the bolt are up to three inches off-grain, feel the hand of the fabric. If it has a stiff finish, it is unlikely you will be able to straighten the grain. If the fabric is soft and pliable, you will most likely get the grain realigned with little effort. If the fabric is more than three inches off, you should reconsider buying it. Finishing standards find fabric that is two to three inches off-grain still acceptable. If it says on the bolt the fabric is perma-press, it will be very difficult to straighten.

Realigning Fabric Grain

Many people believe that by pulling the fabric bias in the opposite direction it is off, they can straighten the fabric. But if you really examine a piece of fabric to which this has been done, you will see that the yarns are now misaligned and pulled out of square. Two better ways to realign the fabric grain are to press a new center fold into the fabric or to make a straightening "pin-frame."

To press a new center fold, start by tearing each end of the yardage to find the crosswise grain. Next, dampen the fabric (with a spray bottle). If you are prewashing or preshrinking the fabric, you can do this step while the fabric is damp. The sizing must be damp in order to allow the yarns to move back to their original position. Fold the fabric in half lengthwise and pin each torn edge together evenly. Then pin the selvages together. Work in short yardages of about ½ yard when doing this. If you can work with a partner, it is helpful. If one holds the fabric at the selvage corners and the other pulls at each end at the center fold, you will see the fabric realign. Now press a new center fold, working from the torn edge and selvage down to the new fold. Once this is complete, turn the fabric over and press the other side, checking for folds and distortion. Then, fold the fabric in half lengthwise again. Check to see that the torn edges again align. If not, repeat the process. Up to a ½" variance is acceptable here.

When fabric tears unevenly, the grain needs to be realigned before cutting.

Realigned torn edges are ready to cut.

A **pin-frame** is a wooden square frame made from 1" x 1"s or 2" x 2"s, using rigid corner braces. Artists' canvas stretchers are a good starting point for getting a pin-frame. This is the most accurate way to correct grain problems.

Pin the cloth exactly even with the grain in the warp and filling directions. Spray or steam until wet, then let dry. The fabric will be squared up when removed from the frame.

For years quilters have been told that grain doesn't really matter in quiltmaking. I would challenge this by having you look closely at the problems in many of the quilts hanging in quilt shows across the country. Borders are stretched and uneven, tops do not lay flat, and corners are stretched out of square. The basics of quiltmaking should include learning about grainline and its effect on the quilt, and then taking the time to straighten and correct grain problems in the fabrics you are working with for the best possible results in your quilts.

CHAPTER 10

THREAD

Yarn is the generic name for an assemblage of fibers that are laid or twisted together and used in the manufacturing of fabric. Yarns are classified as:

- spun yarn, made of staple fiber (like cotton), or
- continuous filament yarn, made of filament fiber (like polyester).

Thread is a product used to join pieces of fabric together to create a textile product. A spun yarn is turned into a thread if it is given considerable twist by doubling, twisting, winding, and in some cases, gas singeing. Following is a list of terms associated with thread and its production:

- **Staple:** Natural fibers or cut lengths from filaments. The staple length of natural fibers varies from less than one inch with some cotton fibers to several feet for some hard fibers. Man-made staple fibers are cut to a specific length (from 8 inches down to about 1½ inches) so that they can be processed on cotton, woolen, or worsted yarn spinning systems.
- **Ply:** The number of single yarns twisted together to form a plied yarn, or the number of plied yarns twisted together to form cord. Also, an individual yarn in a ply yarn or cord.
- **Roll:** The tendency of thread to roll to the right or left during stitching, causing the stitch to appear crooked. Poor-quality threads are likely to roll.
- **Twist:** The number of turns about its axis per unit of length of a yarn, often expressed as turns per inch.

Thread is usually made of plied construction, and is fine, even, and strong. A satisfactory thread must have high strength and adequate elasticity, a smooth surface, dimensional stability, and resistance to snarling or damage by friction, as well as an attractive appearance.

SPUN YARNS

Cotton thread is made by mechanical spinning. Mechanical spinning consists of a series of operations designed to clean and parallel staple fibers, draw them out into a fine strand, and twist them to make a spun yarn. Mechanical spinning is one of the oldest manufacturing processes, and has proven to be an invention as important as the wheel.

Primitive spinning consisted of simply twisting the fibers between the fingers. Later, fibers were bound to a stick called a distaff, which was held under the arm, leaving the fingers free to draw out the fibers. When the strand was about a yard long, the free end was fastened to a rock or spindle, which had enough weight to help twist the yarn. This worked well for wool and flax, but the short cotton fibers would break under the weight of the spindle.

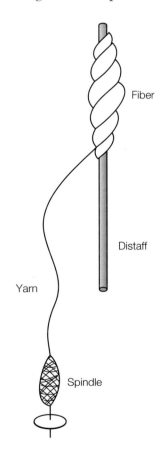

Distaff and spindle

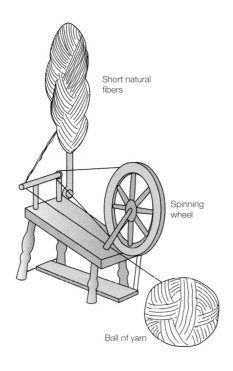

Short natural fibers

Spinning wheel

Ball of yarn

Spinning wheel

The spinning wheel was developed in India by spinners who turned the spindle in a horizontal position and attached it to a wheel, which was then turned by a foot pedal. This was introduced to Europe in the fourteenth century.

By the eighteenth century the factory system had begun. In 1764 James Hargreaves invented the spinning jenny, a machine that turned more than one spinning wheel at a time. As time passed other improvements were made, until power-operated machines made mass production of textiles possible. Today the basic principles of spinning are the same as when man first made yarn.

The steps in spinning staple fiber into yarn are designed to clean and parallel the fibers, draw them out into a fine strand, and twist them to give strength to the finished yarn. This process goes through the following steps:

1. opening: loosens, blends, and cleans the fibers
2. carding: cleans, straightens, and forms sliver
3. combing: straightens, removes short fibers, and forms sliver
4. drawing: parallels, blends, reduces size, and forms sliver
5. roving: reduces size, forms roving with slight twist
6. spinning: twists, winds finished yarn on a bobbin
7. winding: rewinds yarn from bobbin to spool or cone

Each of these processes is discussed in detail in Chapter 2.

Twist

Twist is defined as the spiral arrangement of the fibers around the axis of the yarn. This is achieved by revolving one end of a fiber strand while the other end is held stationary. Twist binds the fibers together and gives the yarn strength.

The amount of twist in the final yarn is identified as low, medium, or high, and varies with the length of the fibers, the size of the yarn, and the intended use. Increasing the amount of twist, up to a certain point, will increase the strength of the yarns. Too much twist places the fibers at right angles to the axis of the yarn, causing a shearing action between fibers, and the yarn loses strength.

Low twist

High twist

Yarns with long fibers do not require as much twist as yarns with short fibers, since they establish more points of contact per fiber and give stronger yarn for the same amount of twist. Fine yarns require more twist than coarse yarns.

Low-twist yarns are used in filling yarns of fabrics that are to be napped. The low twist permits the napping machine to tease out the ends of the staple fibers and create the soft fuzzy surface.

Medium-twist yarns are made from staple fibers. This medium twist gives warp yarns the maximum strength necessary for the high tension they are under on the loom. They must also resist wear caused by the abrasion of the shuttle moving back and forth. The lower twist of filling yarns makes them softer and less apt to kink.

High-twist yarns have up to 30–40 twists per inch. This makes for a very compact and hard yarn, which is used in making voile.

The direction of the twist is described as S-twist (twisted to the right) and Z-twist (twisted to the left). A yarn has S-twist if, when held in vertical position, the spirals are the same as the slope of the central portion of the letter "S." A yarn has a Z-twist if the spirals conform to the slope of the central portion of the letter "Z." Roll a strand of thread toward you with one thumb and finger. A left twist will tighten; a right twist will loosen.

In order to avoid complete untwisting of the finished sewing thread, S-twist is used in the spinning process and Z-twist in the twisting process. Most American threads are twisted to the right (S-twist) giving average results. These threads have a tendency to roll to the right or left during stitching, which causes the stitch to appear slightly crooked. Poor quality threads are more likely to roll.

Most commercial and imported threads are twisted to the left (Z-twist) giving above average results. Left twist resists rolling and makes a larger loop which reduces skipped stitches. Home sewing machines require Z-twisted thread for top performance.

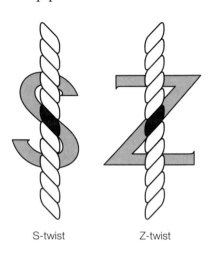

S-twist   Z-twist

The balance of yarns is another important factor concerning twist. If yarns are balanced, the twist has been inserted in such a way that a length of yarn will hang in a loop without kinking or doubling on itself. Unbalanced yarns have enough twist that the yarn will untwist and retwist in the opposite direction, leaving it twisted upon itself.

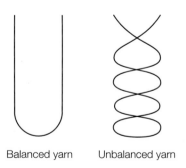

Balanced yarn   Unbalanced yarn

Smooth fabrics require balanced yarns; textured fabrics like crepe can be created from unbalanced yarns.

HOW THREAD IS MADE

Thread is created by twisting more than one yarn together, creating a ply yarn. A single yarn is made from one twisting operation that is performed by the spinning machine.

A single yarn

A ply yarn is made by a second twisting operation that combines two or more singles. Each part of the yarn is called a ply. The twist is inserted by a machine called a twister. Most ply yarns are twisted in the opposite direction to the twist of the singles they are made of. Plying increases the diameter, strength, and quality of the yarn.

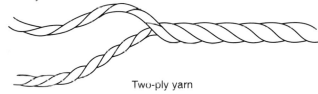

Two-ply yarn

A cord is made by a third twisting operation that twists ply yarns together. Some types of sewing threads and some ropes are made in this manner.

FILAMENT YARNS

Silk is the only natural filament fiber; all others are man-made.

Chemical spinning produces man-made filament fiber, filament yarn, and filament tow. (Filament tow is made into staple and is processed by mechanical spinning, like cotton.) This is a process where a polymer solution is extruded through a spinneret, solidified in fiber form, and the individual filaments immediately brought together, with or without a slight twist, to make the yarn. It is then wound on a bobbin.

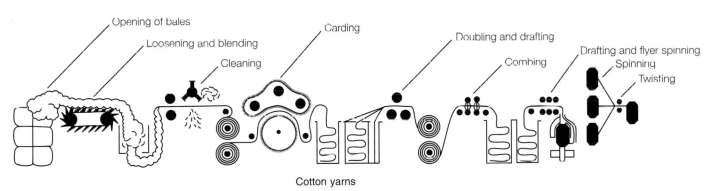

Cotton yarns

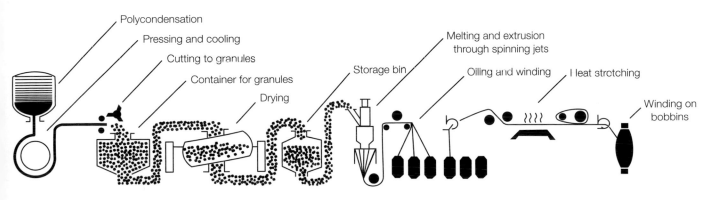

Filament yarns

Before the twentieth century the only continuous filament yarn was silk. All utility fabrics were made with yarns containing staple fibers. However, man-made continuous filament yarns developed in the 1940s made the silk-like fabrics available for the general public.

With the introduction of polyester fabric, polyester threads were needed for strength and stretchability. These fabrics and threads overtook the market, making 100% cotton thread very difficult to obtain. Today, with the increasing demand for natural fibers, cotton thread is once again in demand, and much more readily available.

Yarn is used in the manufacturing of fabric....Thread is a product used to join pieces of fabric together to create a textile product.

THREAD COMPATIBILITY

Why should quilters be concerned about which thread they use in their quilts? The answer has to do with thread strength and fiber compatibility. There are two guidelines to keep in mind when deciding on thread for a project:

- Threads and fabrics you use in the same project should be of like fibers; for example, natural fabrics should be sewn with natural threads, synthetics fabrics should be sewn with synthetic threads; or
- The thread needs to be weaker than the fabric. If the thread is too strong, it can cut or weaken the fabric in the seam. If a thread breaks in a seam it can be mended; if a fabric is cut, it cannot.

Mercerized cotton thread is strong, smooth, lustrous, and resists shrinkage. Size 50, 3-ply is a medium-diameter thread, and is suitable for all hand and machine sewing on light and medium-weight natural fabrics.

Synthetic threads provide strength and elasticity needed for sewing on knit, stretch, bonded, synthetic, and permanent-press fabrics. Polyester/cotton thread combinations consist of cotton-wrapped polyester yarns. These yarns are then plied and twisted together. The cotton sheath provides resistance to heat and makes the thread sew and look more like cotton, while the polyester core gives strength and elasticity.

Silk thread is good for basting and stitching fabrics containing animal fibers. With properties congenial to both silk and wool, it combines durability with elasticity, and leaves no lint or fuzz.

Sizing Systems

When we buy thread, we are used to selecting according to the color, but the sizing is often a mystery. We run across numbers that may or may not mean anything to us, such as 30, 40/3, 60/2, etc. These numbers tell us the thickness of the thread and the number of plies. The higher the first number, the finer the thread. The number behind the slash indicates how many plies are twisted together. This system can be used to determine how fine the thread is and for what purposes it can be used.

Cotton sewing threads are numbered using the English numbering system, sometimes indicated by "Ne." The English numbering tells you how many skeins, at 840 yards each, weigh an English pound. For example, 60 count thread means that 60 skeins, with 840 yards each, weigh one pound.

The metric system tells you how many meters of thread weigh one gram. Nm 100 means that 100 meters of thread weigh one gram. Synthetic thread manufacturers usually use this method, since synthetic thread is a petroleum product and there are no bales to weigh or measure.

In the 1950s a new system to designate yarn size was developed, known as the Tex system. It was intended to replace all the existing count and denier systems with a single system for designating all yarn sizes. However, the Tex system has not been widely accepted and is in limited use in the textile industry. The Tex system is a direct numbering system in which higher Tex numbers correspond to increasingly heavier (thicker) yarns. The Tex standard is 1,000 meters per gram.

If you're curious about how cotton thread sizes compare to synthetic thread sizes, use the following conversion formula. To convert a size from metric to English, use the factor 1.695. For example: 100/1.695=60. To convert a size from English to metric, use the factor 0.591. For example: 60/0.591=100.

Comparison Table of the Most Commonly Used Sewing Thread Counts

Cotton	Ne	20/3	corresponds to	Nm	30/3
	Ne	40/3	"	Nm	70/3
	Ne	50/3	"	Nm	85/3
	Ne	60/3	"	Nm	100/3
	Ne	60/2 or 50/2	"	Nm	100/2
Synthetic	Nm	30/3	corresponds to	Ne	20/3
	Nm	70/3	"	Ne	40/3
	Nm	100/3	"	Ne	60/3

CHAPTER 11

TYPES OF THREADS AND THEIR USES

IMPORTANT FACTORS IN THREAD SELECTION

Sewing is commonly done with thread that is thicker than the fibers which make up the weave of the fabric. This results in a hard seam and often makes the fabric pucker. It is preferable to use a relatively fine thread and smaller stitches than a thread that is too thick and stitches that are too long.

Thread strength should be less than that of the fabric which has been sewn.

Thread Size

Thread size should be as fine as possible but consistent with the strength requirements of the job. Finer threads tend to become buried below the surface of the fabric and are subject to less abrasion than seams sewn with heavier thread, which lay on top of the fabric. Finer threads also require smaller needles, which produce less fabric distortion than heavier needles. The preferred thread size for sewing cotton quilting fabrics is 50/3. The 50 designates the thickness of the thread, or the weight and diameter. The 3 indicates the number of plies twisted together. A 60/3 thread is another excellent thread for piecing. It is lighter in weight and smaller in diameter than 50/3, but is very difficult if not impossible to obtain in the United States. The higher the first number, the finer the thread. The more plies, the stronger the thread.

Thread Strength

Thread strength should be less than that of the fabric which has been sewn. Authorities agree that the seam should be about 60% of the fabric strength. The reason for this is that if excessive stress is placed on a seam, the seam will break instead of the fabric. Seams are easily repaired, but fabric is not. So cotton thread is weaker than the cotton fabric we use, but polyester thread is not. Polyester thread has tiny, abrasive edges that work as saw blades against the soft cotton fibers and will cut through the seams over time. Mercerized cotton thread is treated to make it stronger, more lustrous, and more stable than soft cotton thread.

When purchasing cotton thread, unroll a length and check for quality. A fuzzy thread is made from short fibers, rendering it weak and giving it poor sewing properties. A thread with few fuzzy ends is made from long staple fibers. When twisted, the ends are secured, making it a much stronger thread. This thread will sew a nicer seam and last longer in the item in which it is sewn.

Needle Size

When sewing, the relationship between the needle and thread is critical. If the needle eye is too small for the thread to pass through, the thread will fray and break, and stitches will be skipped. If the needle hole is too big for the thread, the needle and thread will leave a weak and unsightly seam. Below is a chart that gives corresponding needle and thread sizes. This will assist you in choosing a needle for the thread size and fabric weight you are sewing.

Quick Needle/Thread Reference Chart								
Needle Size	60	65	70	75	80	90	100	110
Ultra fine 80/2	•	•						
Nylon monofilament	•	•	•	•	•			
Fine machine embroidery thread 60/2		•	•	•				
DMC® machine embroidery thread 50/2		•	•	•				
Embroidery thread 30/2			•	•	•			
Merc. cotton sewing thread 50/3				•		•		
Synthetic sewing thread (spun)				•	•			
Cotton-wrapped polyester						•		
Cotton 40/3						•	•	
Buttonhole (cordonnet)							•	•

FABRIC, THREAD, AND NEEDLE COMPATIBILITY

Delicate Fabrics:
chiffon, gauze, georgette, organdy, organza, voile

Threads:
80/2, 60/2, 50/2 mercerized cottons, silk, extra-fine polyester

Needle Sizes:
60/8, 65/9, 70/10 universal points

Lightweight Fabrics:
nylon lingerie, batiste, chiffon, dress weight, tricot, organdy, sheer crepe voile

Threads:
60/2, 50/2, 50/3 mercerized cottons, silk, extra-fine cotton-wrapped polyester

Needle Sizes:
65/9, 70/10, 75/11 universal points

Light/Medium-weight Fabrics:
challis, chambray, cotton blends, gingham, jersey, percale, pima cotton, satin, seersucker, taffeta, wool crepe

Threads:
50/3 mercerized cotton, all-purpose polyester

Needle Sizes:
75/11, 80/12 universal point

Medium-weight Fabrics:
broadcloth, chintz, corduroy, flannel, muslin, quilting cottons, taffeta, velveteen, wool flannel

Threads:
50/3 mercerized cotton, all-purpose polyester

Needle Size:
80/12 universal point

Medium/Heavyweight Fabrics:
coating, duck, felt, fleece, gabardine, lightweight denim, linen, quilted fabrics, terry cloth, velvet

Threads:
50/3, 40/3 mercerized cottons

Needle Sizes:
80/12, 90/14 universal point

Heavyweight Fabrics:
canvas, coating, denim, drapery fabric, sailcloth, upholstery

Threads:
50/3, 40/3 mercerized cottons, all-purpose polyester, upholstery

Needle Sizes:
90/14, 100/16, 110/18 universal points, 90/14, 100/16 jeans needle

SEWING THREAD APPLICATIONS

THREAD	APPLICATION	SEWING TECHNIQUE
Polyester Sewing Threads		
Nm 100/3	synthetic fabrics blended fabrics jersey tricot knitwear silk	straight stitch zigzag elastic seams machine buttonhole sewing by hand
Nm 70/3	synthetic fabrics blended fabrics jersey heavy tricot knitwear leather decorator fabrics	straight stitch inside leg seam highly-elastic seams decorative seams
Nm 30/3 (Cordonnet)	synthetic fabrics blended fabrics wool leather tents home textiles	decorative seams (jeans) sewing on buttons sewing on curtain rings sashiko quilting
Cotton Sewing Threads		
Ne 50/3	cotton wool linen jeans	straight stitch zigzag decorative seams for fine fabrics sewing by hand hand made buttonholes
Ne 40/3	cotton wool linen jeans	straight stitch zigzag decorative seams sewing by hand hand-made buttonhole
Ne 60/2	cotton blended fabric wool linen silk synthetic fabrics	darning mending running stitch overlocking blind stitch machine buttonhole appliqué work machine embroidery heirloom sewing
Ne 30/2	For all fabrics suitable for embroidering silk-chiffon	machine embroidery sewing of very fine fabrics blanket stitch appliqué

TYPES OF THREAD

Cotton Thread

Mercerized 3-ply cotton threads are considered the best general sewing thread, and are recommended by most machine specialists. It is strong, smooth, lustrous, and resists shrinkage. Size 50/3 thread is suitable for all hand and machine sewing on light to medium-weight fabrics. Cotton thread has very little thread drag, which keeps tension consistent. Size 40/3 thread is intended for heavier or bottom weight fabrics. Size 40/3 quilting thread is generally not suitable for machine quilting. It requires a large needle, resulting in poor tension and needle holes. Avoid using glazed or waxed quilting threads on your machine, as the finish wears off over time and causes serious tension problems.

Mercerized 2-ply cotton threads are ideal for decorative sewing, embroidery and appliqué, and they come in brilliant colors. You will find 60, 50, and 30 weight two-ply threads.

Cotton/Polyester Thread

Cotton-wrapped polyester is intended to give a slight amount of stretch when sewing blends. Polyester core fibers are individually wrapped with a cotton sheath, then the three plies are twisted together. This thread provides a higher resistance to heat than 100% polyester and gives a cotton appearance, while providing a slight amount of stretch. Problems occur when the needle size is not appropriate for the thread and the sheath is stripped away. Thread seesaws through the eye of a needle up to forty-seven times before being sewn into a stitch. If the needle eye is too small, the thread will be damaged by this process. Cotton-wrapped polyesters tend to "peel" up the length of the thread before it gets to the eye—a condition caused by a too-small needle eye. The smallest needle that should be used with these threads is a 90/14. This needle is most often too heavy for quiltmaking fabrics.

Polyester Thread

Polyester thread is designed to stretch when a knit fabric is expanded, enabling a straight stitch machine to sew knits. When buying polyester thread, buy only the highest quality! This thread has a hard and abrasive finish, not suitable for soft cotton fabrics. It also has a tendency to roll and untwist during use. Low heat resistance and high thread drag make it inappropriate for quiltmaking projects. When low-quality thread has been used a lot, a buildup of film on a machine's thread guides and tension disks can cause erratic tension and looping. Careful cleaning of these areas with soft cotton yarn or a pipe cleaner dipped in lighter fluid will eliminate this buildup.

Nylon Thread

Nylon thread is relatively new to quiltmaking. Since 1986 when I introduced it to the quilt world, this thread has been used extensively. It provides many opportunities to machine quilters, but does require care when purchasing. Not just any nylon will do.

You want to look for nylon thread that is very fine, but stretchy. It should break easier than 50/3 cotton thread. Two very favorable brands are Sew Art International® and YLI Wonder Thread®. Both of these threads are .004 mm in size, and come in clear and smoke. Please take time to look for these threads. Other nylons are either too strong, too weak, or too brittle for quiltmaking. The wrong nylon thread can cut and damage fabrics, and even wear grooves into sewing machine parts. You can obtain very good results by using cotton in the bobbin and nylon in the top of the machine.

Rayon and Metallic Thread

As machine quilting becomes more popular, different threads are being used with great imagination. Metallic and rayon threads add sparkle and shine to quilt stitches. However, they have very low resistance to abrasion, and are therefore not suitable for a finished product that will receive rough or heavy use. They are most suitable for decorative purposes, as in garments, wall quilts, and fiber art quilts.

Embroidery and metallic needles are now available to accomodate the specific requirements of these threads. The embroidery needle has a deep groove down the front of the needle, a large eye, similar to a topstitching needle, and special finishes. These features protect the rayon thread from excessive friction during the stitching process, elimination breakage, and weakening of the thread. When using metallic threads, using special metallic needles is recommended.

More on Thread

Remember the importance of planning wisely when purchasing thread. Try to use only fresh, high-quality thread. Old threads, of any fiber content, break down and change their characteristics as they age. This results in more fraying, more lint shedding, breakage, and weak seams. To test your thread, pull on a strand. Old thread and even new thread that is of poor quality will break easily.

THE PRICE OF THREAD

Good thread is expensive—but if you stop and think about what you are making, you quickly realize it is worth the money. Consider the following scenario. You determine you will need 10 spools of thread for a project. A high-quality thread is $1.90 a spool, which you think

is too expensive. You find a lower priced (and much lower quality) thread, at say 99¢ a spool. At 99¢ a spool you will spend $9.99 for your thread. If you purchased the higher priced thread, you would have spent $19.00—a savings of $9.01. If you consider what you spent for the fabrics in the project, the batting, the time you are putting into the project, and how long you expect the quilt to last, you must ask yourself: Will cheap thread hold up over the long run in the seams? Will the quilt hold together for many decades? The answer is: no. Isn't your time and effort worth the very best products you can buy? Is $9.01 that much when you look at the big picture? You might think about this when purchasing fabric and batting, too.

TROUBLESHOOTING STITCHING PROBLEMS

Machine Stitching

- If you are having problems with tension or general stitch quality, it could be that your machine needle is inserted improperly. The needle "scarf" should be to the back, the groove to the front.
- Sew some test seams on fabric scraps before stitching the project. Check needle size and stitch tension and length, making any adjustments necessary.
- As a general rule, shorten stitches for lightweight fabrics, lengthen stitches for heavier fabrics.
- Don't use poor-quality "bargain" thread. It is prone to breaking and knotting.
- Don't force fabric through your machine by pulling. Let the feed system do the work for you.

General Problems with Machine Stitching

Problem:

Skipped machine stitches—top thread doesn't form a loop with the bobbin thread

Solution:

- Use the same thread in the top and bottom, if possible.
- Thread the machine correctly.
- Change needles. Special banded needles have a longer scarf so they pick up the bobbin thread more easily. Also experiment with different sizes, points and specialty needles.
- Change to a straight stitch throat plate (only for straight stitching).

Problem:

Puckered seams and edges

Solution:

- Adjust and balance tension.
- Change to a new, smaller needle.
- Seal the seam; press flat, then press open or to one side.
- If available, adjust the "pressure regulator" which alters the amount of pressure on the foot.
- Shorten stitch length to 12–15 stitches/inch for lighter weight fabrics. Shorter stitches use more thread. Puckers can be caused by too little thread and tight tension.

Problem:

Machine is eating the fabric—pushing it down into the throat plate

Solution:

- Change to a straight stitch throat plate (only for straight stitching).
- Start stitching right at the fabric edge by holding onto the thread tail. Pull taut as you begin to stitch.
- For most lightweight fabrics, it is best not to backstitch at the very beginning and end of the seams, as jamming can occur. Instead, simply shorten the stitch length to 15 - 18 stitches per inch at these points.

Hand Stitching

- Keep in mind that hand needles are available in a range of sizes (1 – 12, 12 being the finest). The thread you are using might be too large for the needle eye.
- A fine, short needle is best for short single stitches. Longer needles can be used for long basting stitches.
- Keep thread length short for easier handling and less twisting.
- Another way to prevent twisting is to thread the needle with the end cut from the spool. If twisting does occur, let the needle dangle and straighten with your forefingers by sliding down the thread length.

CHAPTER 12

BATTING

Before a pieced or appliquéd quilt top becomes a quilt, it has to be made into a sandwich which introduces a filler between the top and back. This filler is held in place by quilting stitches. Now we have a quilt. Batting, also known as wadding or filling, is one of the most essential parts of a quilt. Without it, there is no "quilt."

HISTORY OF BATTING

Before manufactured batting was available, people produced their own batting at home. Small amounts of unspun cotton or wool were carded into batts. These small batts were laid side by side to cover the quilt lining, then the top was carefully placed on top and the three layers were very closely quilted together. The most common and preferred fiber was cotton, but many antique quilts were made with wool, silk, flax, woven blankets (generally wool), or worn-out quilts as batting.

Batting has been used in one form or another throughout the centuries. Much of the dating of antique quilts has been done by studying the battings. The invention of the cotton gin marks a very important time to a quilt collector. With the introduction of the cotton gin you began to see more seeds in the quilt fillers. Prior to this quilt battings were made from cotton picked by slave labor. Their fingers did a better job than the early machines. Quilts made in the first quarter of the nineteenth century had many seeds. Later improvements to the cotton gin led to fewer and fewer seeds. A quilt batting with as many as two or three seeds to the square inch dates the quilt to around 1830. A quilt batting with a seed or two every few inches suggest the quilt was made in approximately the 1850s. Between 1840 and 1860 quilting was so popular women were

demanding adequate products for their quilts. They wanted the best grade of filler available, with very few seeds. Today, you see some cotton battings with small seed chips.

Be careful when using these batts in white or very light-colored quilts. Not only can the dark specks show through the top fabric, but if any oil is in the chip, it has the potential to stain the fabric. These batts are intended to be used with muslin and medium to dark fabrics.

Early Batting Manufacturers

One of the first companies to produce batting commercially was Stearns and Foster of Cincinnati. George S. Stearn and Seth C. Foster perfected a method of producing cotton batting in the mid-1840s. They discovered how to glaze sheets of cotton for easier handling by coating a slab of marble with starch paste (which came from a small local company called Procter and Gamble), laying a web of cotton on it, and then peeling it off. The result was hung on a clothes line to dry. Reportedly, production was rather slow.

In the same year Elias Howe patented the sewing machine. The population of Los Angeles was 1,610, there were no automobiles, no electric lights, no radios, no child labor laws, and the average working day was thirteen to fifteen hours for adults.

Stearns and Foster also produced wadding, which was generally thicker and used in clothing as well as upholstery. The names of their products were influenced by the country's development: Homestead, Boone, Victoria, Economy, and of course Mountain Mist. The

Stearns and Foster Company was also one of the very first manufacturers of polyester quilt batting (in 1956) using duPont polyester. Morning Glory and Fairfield were next on the scene, and now we have numerous companies promoting quilt battings of every description.

My Personal Interest in Batting

My personal interest in batting started in 1983 when I purchased an old farm house. I needed antique quilts to decorate the house. After learning that all the family quilts I grew up with were either gone or worn past repair, I realized that if I was going to get the quilts I wanted in the house, I would have to make them myself. With the guidance of my mother, I started to experiment with 100% Natural Cotton® from Mountain Mist. That and Fairfield Cotton Classic® were the only cotton battings on the market at that time.

It was surprisingly difficult to obtain the cotton, and when I did find it, I was regularly warned that cotton's excessive shrinkage, wadding, and tearing could ruin my quilt. But the whole point was that the shrinkage was the look I was after, and polyester certainly wasn't going to give my new quilts an old look. This started my quest for battings that would give my quilts a distinct look, not just a filling to put between the layers of the quilt.

Machine quilting was another factor affecting my choice of battings. I found that polyester battings would stretch, slide, and distort, making it very difficult to machine quilt. Cottons, on the other hand, would stick tightly to the fabric layers, making it considerably easier to quilt under the machine. I started recommending cotton to my machine quilting students, and they were getting much better results than the beginners did with polyester. With the growing popularity of machine quilt-ing, cotton batting became more popular. This is one way machine quilting shook the industry. I am glad I pushed cotton so much back then. It has led to the variety of products available to us today.

Once I started to investigate the battings on the market, I lectured about making choices based on the quilts' needs, not shop owners', teachers', or authors' opinions and preferences. I felt quiltmakers needed to choose the look they envisioned for their finished quilts and experiment with different battings, using them in different ways.

Many quilters have asked how in the world I can do a two-hour lecture on batting! I could talk about batting with enthusiasm for even longer than that, and get you excited, too. To me, batting is what makes a quilt, not the pretty fabric and choice of design. If you understand batting, your quilts will reflect this in their durability and beauty.

Knowing how to test battings is one thing, understanding how they are manufactured and why they are not "perfect" is another. This chapter will walk you through the manufacturing processes commonly used in producing batts today. It will explain how to choose a batt based on its characteristics and on what it will do for the quilt, not on the brand name or fiber content.

Batting is defined in the dictionary as "fibers wadded into sheets." This doesn't bring to mind a very pleasing product, does it? Batting, which used to be called wadding, is further defined as "any soft material for use in padding, packing, stuffing, etc., especially cotton made into loose, fluffy sheets." Sounds a little better. The textile industry's definition is a soft, bulky assembly of fibers, usually carded. A carded web is sometimes called a batt.

Batting is technically known as a nonwoven fabric. A nonwoven fabric is defined as "an assemblage of fibers held together by mechanical, chemical, or thermal means, resulting in a mechanically stable, self-supporting, and generally flexible, web-like structure."

The process of manufacturing nonwovens is different than for woven or knitted fabrics, as it is generally made directly from raw materials, eliminating conventional textile operations such as carding, roving, spinning, and weaving or knitting. Nonwoven manufacturing involves selecting the fiber or raw material, forming the web, web consolidation, and web finishing.

The fibers used in the production of quilt battings are polyester, cotton, wool, and silk.

TYPES OF FIBERS USED IN BATTINGS

Polyester Battings

Polyester is a synthetic polymer known technically as polyethylene terephthalate. Polyester is a man-made fiber, providing uniformity and consistency of supply which cannot be equaled readily by natural fibers. The polymer is extruded through a spinneret, which produces a uniform filament. The size of the filament is referred to as denier. Denier is rated on a numbering system of fineness. The lower the number, the finer the fiber; the higher the number, the coarser the fiber. The lower the denier, the softer, finer, and more drapable the finished product will be. The higher the denier, the stiffer, coarser, and harder the fiber. Most polyester quilt battings are made with 6–12 denier fiber. Some new polyester battings are made with 3 denier fiber, making them much softer and finer than before.

The finer the fiber, the more fibers it takes to fill a given space and the more crossovers and bonding points you will have. The larger the

fiber, the less fibers it takes to fill the same space, and the fewer crossovers and bonding points you will have. This is important to a quilter, since each bonding point secures the fibers, and the more bonding points there are, the stronger the batting is and the less chance bearding will occur. The problem for manufacturers is that the more you lower the denier of the fiber, the more difficult it is to process.

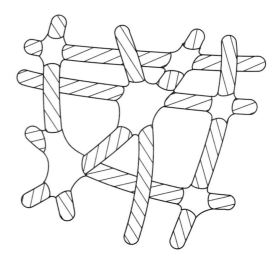

Crossover bonding points

Polyester can be physically modified by the crimping and finishing processes. In the crimping process, a crimp is applied to the fiber as it is extruded. The crimp and denier determine the bulk and loft of the fiber. Generally, high crimp gives more bulk and loft to the fiber. When the fiber is crimped, it is cut to the desired length (of up to two inches). Again, the longer the fiber, the less chance there is for fiber migration or bearding.

Polyester fibers can also be finished to change the way they behave. One example is the siliconized fibers used by Hobbs Bonded Fibers in their Poly-Down® polyester batting. This process enhances the washability, drape, and ease of quilting. It gives the fibers a very soft hand. When the finished quilt is washed, the batting resists water, making it lighter and less stressful on the quilting stitches.

Siliconizing is also an expensive process which makes the fiber more difficult to run through the machinery. Not all siliconized fibers can be easily bonded. Getting the fiber to behave properly for manufacturing processes is a balancing act. Danny Natividad, the chemical engineer at Hobbs Bonded Fibers, calls his job the "artistry of engineering." His quest is to find the right combination of fiber, production method, and finishing processes to make a superior product. Polyester fibers are constantly changing and improving, and dedication by engineers like Danny Natividad result in new, improved polyester battings for our quilts.

Cotton Battings

Cotton fiber has been used for wadding or batting as far back as history records quilting. We lost touch with cotton as a quilt batting during the 1970s and early 1980s, but a renewed interest and desire for the comfort and look of cotton has brought it back into the spotlight.

Cotton is a natural fiber and does not yield the consistency possible with synthetic fiber battings. The color, fineness, and length of the fiber is dependent on the area the cotton is grown, the weather conditions, soil conditions, and chemicals used in farming, as well as other factors. The three cotton properties most often referred to in nonwovens are micronaire, length, and strength. Micronaire and length are the most important factors in batting manufacturing.

Micronaire is an airflow measurement that determines the fineness of the fiber. In a porous chamber 2.34 grams of cotton are compressed to a specific volume. Air is forced through the specimen and the resistance to the airflow is proportional to the linear density of the fibers.

This is expressed in micrograms per inch. The finer the fiber, the better it is for quilt batting.

Fiber length varies according to the type of cotton. Upland raw cotton fibers are normally between 0.9 and 1.2 inches. Pima cotton fibers can be as long as 1.6 inches. In batting manufacturing, the longer the fiber, the more expensive it is. Short fibers make a denser web, and thus have more shrinkage. Short fibers are laid in a random web, generally using an air-lay machine. Binder fibers are often added to create stability. Short fiber batts are more difficult to hand quilt because of the matted, compacted fibers, but do give an antique look to quilts, due to the rattailing and higher compacting. Rattailing is where fibers bunch on the surface of the batt in a long roll. Longer cotton fibers can be carded, making an oriented fiber web. Binder fibers are not as necessary in these batts. Because of the combed fibers, it is easier to hand quilt.

Raw cotton from the gin contains plant materials and field trash not removed by the ginning process. Raw cotton needs to be scoured and in some cases bleached for quilt batting because absorbency, purity, and whiteness is often desired.

Preparing the Cotton: Scouring and Bleaching

In the scouring process the cotton fiber is saturated with a caustic soda (sodium hydroxide) solution. The alkali solution remains on the fiber at elevated temperatures to speed chemical reactions. During this time the natural oils and waxes are saponified (converted into soaps), the plant matter is softened, and pectins and other non-cellulosic materials are suspended so they can be washed away. After a predetermined amount of time to allow for complete scouring, the alkali, saponified waxes, and suspended materials are rinsed away with water. This fiber can then be dried, baled, and shipped out for production of non-bleached products.

If bleaching is desired, a bleaching solution is applied after the scouring process. A stabilized oxidizing agent, hydrogen peroxide or sodium hypochlorite, is used in the bleaching solution to remove the natural coloring and whiten the fiber. In the U.S., hydrogen peroxide is the most widely used agent for bleaching raw cotton in fiber form. The bleaching solution remains on the fiber at elevated temperatures for a fixed amount of time to allow for proper removal of the color. Then the solution is rinsed away. Again, the fiber is dried and baled, ready for manufacturing.

Wool Battings

Wool has been used in quilting for generations. Until recently, commercially-produced wool quilt batts were not readily available.

Wool has characteristics that no other fiber has. First, the wool fiber has built-in barbs, giving it bounce and loft that allow it to always return to its original shape. Wool has a recovery rate from compression of ninety-five percent, which is better than any other fiber. (Polyester averages seventy-three percent, depending on the type of polyester fiber treatment used.)

Today's wool batting is made by blending fibers from different breeds. The fibers average two to three inches long, and have a medium fiber micronaire (average grade of 58 to 60). The finer the wool fiber, the more likely it is to beard.

The wool fiber is first scoured. Thorough scouring removes excess lanolin. This scouring and drying process preshrinks the wool fiber and is often referred to as Superwash. It is then dried, baled, and ready for manufacturing.

Wool is the most forgiving fiber, making it very easy to work with throughout the manufacturing processes.

Silk Battings

At this time, silk is not readily available as a commercially-produced quilt batt. There are a few loose fiber products on the market, but they might not technically be considered batting. We hope to see a silk batt on the market in the future. Silk provides body and drape, and is extremely lightweight, but the high cost of producing silk batts has stemmed extensive production of it.

PROS AND CONS OF EACH BATTING FIBER

The rating system used below ranges from 1–5, with 1 representing the best performance or most expensive, and 5 representing the poorest performance or least expensive.

	Polyester	Cotton	Wool	Silk
Consistency of fiber	1	4	4	3
Washability	2	3[1]	3	3
Shrinkage	1	3	4	--[5]
Warmth (perceived)	1[2]	3	1	2
Ease of quilting	2	3[3]	1	3
Resiliency (rebound)	1–2[4]	5	1	4
Breathability	5	3	2	1
Longevity	4	1	1	3
Price	4–5	3	2	1

1. Washability depends on the quality and type of cotton fiber used. Some cottons wash as well as, if not better than, polyester. The quality of polyester also has to be taken into consideration.

2. Polyester is very warm to some—and extremely hot to others. Polyester does not breathe like wool, therefore it holds the heat next to the body. For some this is the only way to stay warm; to others, the heat is like being wrapped in plastic and is uncomfortable.

3. Some cotton batts are extremely easy to quilt; others are very difficult. This can depend on the length of the fiber as well as the bonding process used, especially if a scrim has been applied.

4. Resiliency depends on the type of fiber used. The newer, finer denier polyesters that are resin bonded with the soft resins now available are much easier to work with than the wiry hard finished batts we used in the past.

5. Information not available at time of writing.

HOW BATTING IS MADE

Formation of Nonwoven Webs

The first consideration is the fiber to be used, or the combination of fibers. A cotton/polyester blend batt or a thermal-bonded batt must be blended so that fiber content is by weight percentages. Obviously, humidity conditions can play a role in this, and often adjustments to the fiber percentages must be altered to enable the fibers to run through the processes correctly.

Once the fiber has been chosen for the finished product, it goes into production. Quilt battings are produced using dry-laid systems. The primary methods of forming web structures using dry-laid technology are carding, garnetting, and air-laying. Before the actual web formation can take place, the fiber must progress through a number of steps including bale opening, blending, and coarse opening.

Dry-laid nonwoven fabrics are made with staple fibers. Regardless of how the end product is bonded or finished, the fiber is chosen (or engineered) to meet the needs of a particular nonwoven fabric. Quilt battings have specific purposes, and as discussed earlier, choosing the fiber is the first step.

Equally important is understanding how the fiber will perform in the opening, blending, and web-forming operations, and knowing how to select equipment accordingly.

The first step of fiber preparation is the mechanical and pneumatic process of handling fibers from the bale to the point where the fiber is introduced into a web-forming machine.

The following processes are included in a typical fiber-preparation line: bale opening, blending, coarse opening, and web-former feeding. The following illustration shows a typical nonwovens line for processing a blend of fibers from the bale to the web-forming equipment.

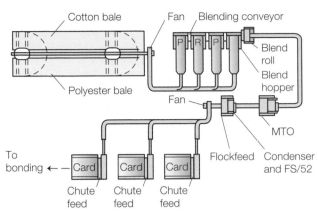

Production line layout of nonwovens. Bale to web forming equipment.

Bale Opening

The bales are unstrapped and placed within reach of the bale opener. Then fibers are placed in the opener to start the opening process.

Bales of fiber waiting to be processed

Unstrapping a bale in preparation for opening

Cotton fiber as it comes from the bale

Opening process

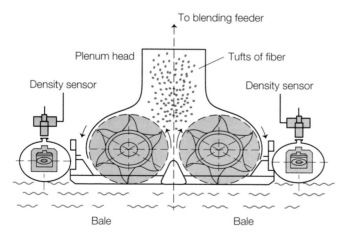
Opening process. Opening rolls create an air vacuum.

The opening heads go back and forth across the bales and start and stop on demand to pick up fiber. In smaller operations this process is done by hand. The bale is opened and the fibers are placed in the blending hopper. The fiber is channeled to the blending hopper, thus keeping the correct supply of fiber in the hoppers to ensure maximum blending. The fibers are carried through a duct by fans that send the fiber to the blending machine on a conveyor belt. The object of an opening line is to reduce the size of fiber tufts from the bale to the web-forming machine. The smaller the size of the tufts, the better the blending will be.

Blending

The blending hopper gently open the tufts of fiber by sending it through a roller embedded with needle bars.

Close-up of opening heads

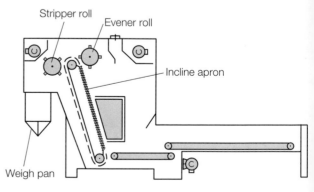
Blend hopper

Blending Hopper

The tufts are then dropped by hoppers into a weigh pan. The hoppers have electronic weight controls that work together so that all of the weigh pans dump simultaneously onto the next conveyor.

Fibers coming from blending hoppers. This is the blending of polyester and cotton in an 80/20 ratio.

Feed apron taking fibers to be opened

Coarse Opening

This process further reduces the tuft size by passing the fiber between rolls A and B and between rolls B and C (see opener illustration). As the fiber passes through these rollers the tufts are reduced in size; the smaller tufts are carried on, while the larger tufts are transferred back for another pass through the same process. The opened fibers are then carried by air stream to the web former.

Coarse opener

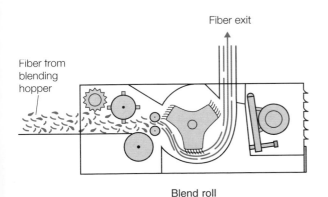

Blend roll

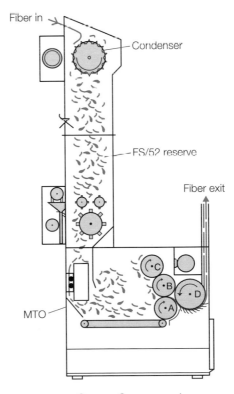

Opener. Coarse opening

Web-former Feeding

Once the fiber is blended and well opened, it can be arranged to feed the web-forming machine. A chute feed can be used for fibers up to 60 mm in length. Longer fibers use a hopper feed.

Chute Feeding

A chute is designed to form a uniform feed mat to feed a web former. Opened fibers are blown into the transition that is located on top of the chute. The fiber is fed into a feed roll and feed plate arrangement, which meters the fiber into the pin beater, provides gentle fiber opening, and prevents fiber damage. The opened fiber is then carried by air, which is introduced at the pin beater roll and feed plate, down into the forming chamber of the chute. Air and mechanical movements help to distribute the fiber evenly in the forming chamber in both the machine direction and cross direction, thus creating a feed mat of uniform consistency to feed the web former.

Hopper Feeding

The opened fiber is transported by air from the last opening point into a condenser that travels back and forth across the filling compartment. This allows for more blending of the fibers as the compartment is filled, and the fibers are metered onto the conveyor by the opener roll. The process of feeding the opened tufts of fiber takes place by means of a spiked apron and the evener roll. Tufts are carried by the inclined apron, and the evener roll levels out the excess fiber.

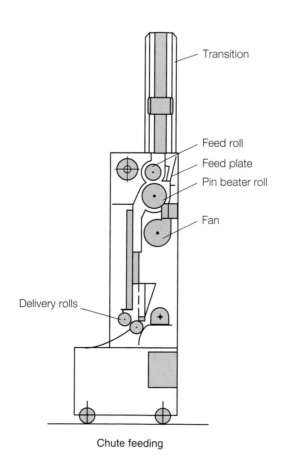

Chute feeding

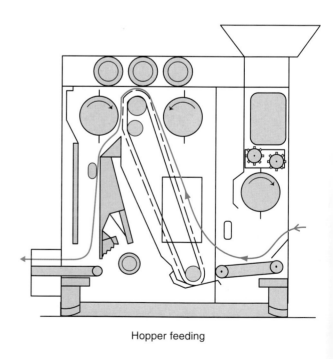

Hopper feeding

FROM FIBER TO FABRIC

Web Formation and Layering

The dry-web processes for making quilt batting are generally mechanical web formations (card or garnett) and aerodynamic web formations (air lay).

Mechanical Web Formations; Carding

A card is a machine designed to separate fibers and remove impurities, then align and deliver the fibers to be laid down as a web or to be further separated and fed to an air-laid process. The fibers in the web are aligned with each other in predominantly the same direction. The machine consists of a series of rolls or a drum covered with many projecting wires or metal teeth. These are rigid, saw-tooth wires that have a specific height, pitch, and angle on the points, which allow for handling many different fibers. These wire-covered rolls and drums are called cards.

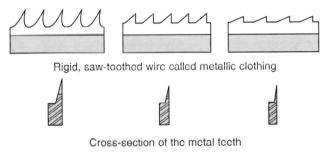

Rigid, saw-toothed wire called metallic clothing

Cross-section of the metal teeth

Before the fiber enters the card, it is entangled and varies in weight throughout the feed mat area. As the fiber is fed into the feed roll, tuft sizes are reduced and the fiber is carded. A stripping action occurs when fiber is transferred from one roll to another with the wire points in the same direction. The difference in the surface speeds allows the transfer of the fiber.

Since these rolls have opposing points, this is a carding action. The fiber tufts are then transferred from the worker to the stripper. The stripper puts the fiber back onto the cylinder,

ahead of the carding plane, which allows the fiber to be reworked again and again until the tufts are reduced to individual fibers.

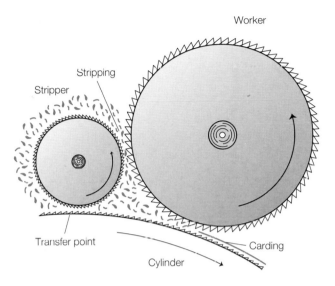

Worker/stripper action

The carding action that takes place within the web former is the combing of fibers between two rolls that have opposing points.

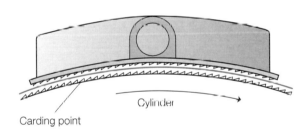

Carding action in web former

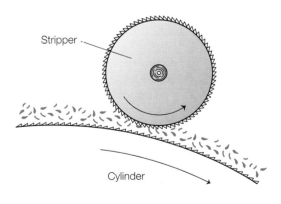

Cleaning fiber out of card

This action occurs when there is a difference in the speed of the opposing surfaces. It is a mechanical action in which the fibers are held by one surface while another surface combs the fibers, which helps to make the fibers parallel before transferring them to the next roll in the web former.

Card

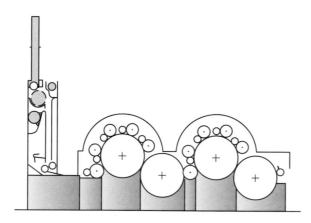

Chute feed and roller top card

The card is the most important part of a nonwovens production line. Up to this point in the process line, fibers have been blended, opened, and formed by the chute feed into a feed mat. The card is required to reduce the tufts to individual fibers, make the fibers parallel, and form a web structure of a precise weight and width at a given line speed.

Feed mat going into the card

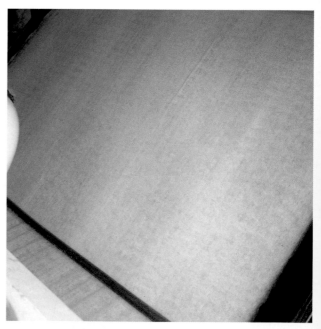

The web formed by the card

Mechanical Web Formations; Garnetting

A garnett is similar to a card. It is a group of rolls placed in an order that allows a given wire configuration, along with certain speed relationships, the ability to level, transport, comb and interlock fibers to form a web.

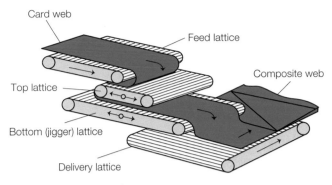

Card web

Feed lattice

Top lattice

Composite web

Bottom (jigger) lattice

Delivery lattice

Crosslapping action

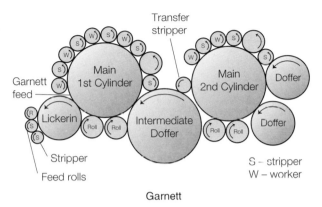

Transfer stripper

Garnett feed

Main 1st Cylinder

Main 2nd Cylinder

Doffer

Lickerin

Intermediate Doffer

Doffer

Roll

Roll

Roll

Roll

Stripper

Feed rolls

S – stripper
W – worker

Garnett

Garnetts are most widely used for processing wadding and pads for the bedding industry. They are also used to produce high-loft products such as comforters. Generally, a garnett will deliver a more random web than a card. Garnetting is used where the evenness of a product is a critical factor and high loft is needed, and for webs that are not going to be bonded.

Layering or Crosslapping

A single layer of carded web is too light and diffuse to make into a fabric, so a number of layers must be laid on top of one another to get the necessary weight. This is called cross layering, or crosslapping. Crosslapping is achieved by folding webs that are formed on cards or garnetts and delivered by a conveyor into the lapper, which continuously transfers the web onto an apron operating at right angles to the crosslayering motion. The crosslapper can be adjusted to allow for width changes in the product line. With crosslapping, the thickness can be controlled by increasing or decreasing the number of layers of webs from the card or garnett. The web is layered onto a floor apron (conveyor) that moves 90° from the input direction.

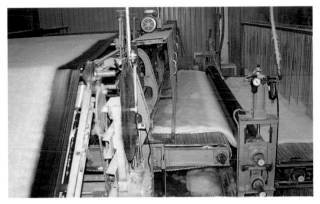

Web being fed to the crosslapper

Crosslapping

Layers of web that are lapped by the crosslapper

Aerodynamic Web Formation; Air-lay

This process produces a random nonwoven web. It is used to produce battings from short lint fibers, among many other things.

The air-laid webs are produced by air-laying or mechanical fiber randomizing processes. The fibers are first suspended in air and then deposited randomly on the conveyor belt or screen. The fiber size is relatively short. The fiber orientation is usually completely random. The air-laid web is then carried to the bonding area.

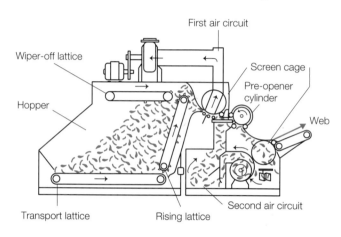

Air-laid web formation technique

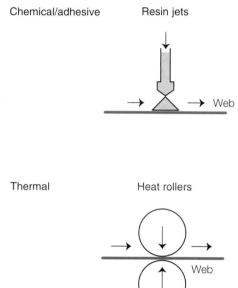

Mechanical — Needleboard — Web

Chemical/adhesive — Resin jets — Web

Thermal — Heat rollers — Web

Web Consolidation and Finishing

Web consolidation or bonding techniques are divided into three generic categories: mechanical, chemical, and thermal. The choice of a particular bonding technique is dictated mainly by the ultimate fabric applications and/or type of web. Occasionally, a combination of two or more techniques is used to achieve bonding, as with Hobbs Heirloom Premium Cotton®, which is needlepunched and chemical bonded.

Mechanical Bonding; Needlepunching

Needlepunching is a process of mechanically entangling a web to form a fabric by puncturing the web with an array of barbed needles that carry tufts of the web's own fibers in a vertical direction through the web.

Barbed felting needle

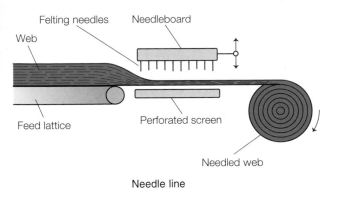

Needle line

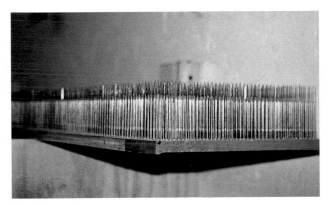

Needleboard

The needles are positioned in a non-aligned arrangement and are designed to release the fiber as the needleboard is withdrawn. A wide range of fabric densities can be achieved by varying the amount of strokes per minute, the rate the web is running through the machine, and the degree of penetration of the needles. The web is made on a web former (card or garnett), crosslapped into a batt, and then fed into the needle loom.

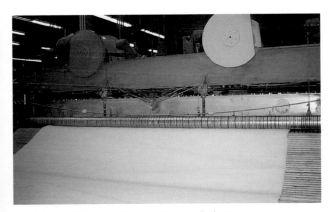

Crosslapped layers going into the needle loom

Close-up of needlepunching action

End view close-up of needle loom in action

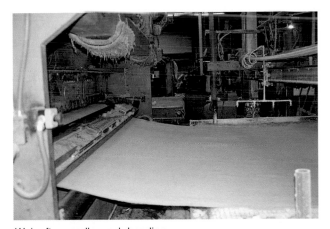

Web after needlepunch bonding

A scrim can be added to the web before needle punching is done. A scrim is a very open fabric, similar to netting or interfacing, that is used as a support for the fiber. The needles penetrate the scrim at the same time as the web, making it an integral part of the finished web.

Battings with scrim added have less stretch and more stability than battings without. Some of these products are very hard, flat, and fairly stiff, while others are soft and resilient. This is dependent on the expectations of the finished product.

Chemical (Resin) Bonding

Bonding a web structure by means of a chemical is one of the most common methods of bonding in the nonwovens industry. It is simply the application of chemical binder and the curing of the binder. The most widely used chemical is latex. Resins are being developed that give a softer hand than before. The amount of bonding agent used on a product can affect its hand. There are trade-offs with the amount of resin used. The higher the resin content, the stiffer but more durable the product. The lower the resin content, the softer but less durable the product. If you use the newer, softer polyester fibers, more resin can be used without losing the soft hand. This is the magic of chemical engineering.

The bonding agent is generally sprayed onto the web, saturated in the web through various means, or printed onto the web. When sprayed, the bonding agent usually stays close to the surface of the material, resulting in a web with little strength, high bulk, and a fair degree of openness. If saturated, the fibers tend to become rigid and stiff, and result in a thinner end product. Print bonding imparts varying degrees of openness, flexibility, breathability, and bulkiness in the unprinted areas. Once the bonding agent is applied, it is cured in ovens to achieve bonding.

Batting is bonded using one of three methods: mechanical, chemical, or thermal.

Spray heads used in chemical (resin) bonding

FROM FIBER TO FABRIC

Web is turned over and sprayed on back side by second set of spray heads.

Thermal Bonding

Thermal bonding is the process of using heat to bond or stabilize a web structure that consists of a thermoplastic fiber. All or part of the fibers act as thermal binders, thus eliminating the use of other types of binders. Binder fibers are specially engineered as low melting-point fibers that are blended with other fibers in a web, so that a uniformly bonded structure can be generated at low temperature by melting of the binder fiber with other fibers at the cross-over points. The fusion is achieved by the direct action of heat and pressure via a calender, an oven, a radiant heat source, or an ultrasonic wave source. The degree of fusion determines many of the web qualities, especially hand and softness.

In air-laid cotton batts a binder fiber of thermoplastic fiber is generally added to the cotton. The binder fiber melts in the calendering process—often referred to as glazing—thus creating a bonding point with the cotton fibers, making the short fiber web easy to handle. Binder fiber is not counted as fiber content. Up to forty percent of the total fiber content of the batt can be this binder fiber (twenty percent is average), but all of this material must be melted and not identifiable under a microscope as a fiber in order to call the end product 100% cotton. When these short fiber batts are washed the cotton tends to lump. This disintegration of the fiber web in the center of the fiber layers is called rattailing.

Once the web is bonded it is taken to the end of the line, where giant rotary cutters trim the edges and cut the batt into desired widths. It is then rolled onto large rolls and stored for future packaging or shipping.

Web leaving oven and heading toward roller

End view of ovens. Bottom layer is first sprayed and enters the oven. Top shows web after it has been turned over and sprayed on the other side, cured, and passed through again.

Giant rotary cutters trim the ends and desired width.

Finished roll: removing trimmed ends

FLAMMABILITY

I cannot talk in detail about batting without addressing the flammability issue. Some of the information about textiles and their performance in a fire situation can be misleading.

Flammable is defined as "easily set on fire." Speaking purely about the fiber, wool is the least flammable fiber available. Firefighters use wool blankets to smother fire when needed. After wool, polyester is the next least flammable. Cotton and silk are the most flammable fibers. Cotton and silk flash at exposure to flame, and burn readily, leaving a charred powdery residue. If exposed to the fire, you will get burned from cotton. But remember, we are not talking about the most dangerous fiber, just the most flammable.

While some polyester battings are less flammable than other polyester battings, all polyester melts when burned and creates worse burns than natural fiber battings.

Polyester fiber generally melts when burned, leaving a tarry, hot liquid that burns into the skin. Consequently synthetic fibers do more damage to flesh than cotton in the same situation. The basic problem is that no matter what batting you put in the quilt, the outside layers are cotton, which is flammable. Therefore, all quilts are flammable if introduced to a flame. For quilters who work with non-flammable fabrics, batting flammability might be a bigger issue.

Another issue that pops up is that some polyesters are less flammable than others. This is not a truly valid issue, as all polyesters melt when burned, and do create the worse burns.

While some polyester battings are less flammable than other polyester battings, all polyester melts when burned and creates worse burns than natural fiber battings.

BATTING FLAMMABILITY TEST

Try the following test if you really want to compare flammability in different types of batting.

Collect several different types of battings, e.g., resin bonded polyester, thermal bonded polyester, cotton/polyester blends, pure cotton, cotton with scrim, and wool. Cover each square with cotton quilting fabric and stitch or staple around all the edges. Put each square, one at a time, into a fire proof container (a metal trash can) and set on fire with a lighter or match. Observe how fast the flame catches and travels and how the batting reacts. Look at the residue once the fire has spent itself. Be very careful not to hold the piece when you start the fire. The flame can travel much faster than you might expect, and if any melting polyester gets on your skin, you could suffer a very bad burn.

Once you try burning different batting, you should have a better idea of which fibers would cause the greatest amount of damage in a fire situation. If this issue is of real concern to you, you will find the safest quilt is wool on the inside and outside.

EXAMINATION OF POPULAR BATTINGS ON THE MARKET TODAY

Instead of going through a detailed description of every batt on the market, I have provided general information on readily available batts in the reference chart on the following page. Start to examine each batt you use and see if you can identify any or all of the manufacturing processes used in their production.

Brand Name	Fiber Content & Bonding Process	Quilting Distance	Appearance
Mountain Mist Blue Ribbon	100% cotton Thermal bonded	Up to 2"	Flat, thin; pure white; antique appearance
Morning Glory Old Fashioned	100% cotton Needlepunched with scrim	4"–6"	Natural color; has some plant residue left in for old look; puckers slightly from shrinkage
Morning Glory Clearly Bleached	100% cotton Needlepunched (no scrim)	1"–6"	Flat, thin, pure white
Morning Glory Clearly Unbleached	100% cotton Needlepunched (no scrim)	1"–6"	Flat, thin; natural color with some plant residue
Mountain Mist 100% Natural Cotton	100% cotton Thermal bonded	1/4"–1"	Pure white; antique appearance; puckers from shrinkage
Warm Products Warm and Natural	100% cotton Needlepunched with scrim	Up to 10"	Very flat and thin; natural color with some plant residue
Fairfield Soft Touch	100% cotton Needlepunched (no scrim)	Up to 2"	Thicker than some needlepunched batts; pure white
Hobbs Organic 100% Cotton	100% organically grown and processed cotton Needlepunched, organic resin bonded	Up to 2"	Natural color; flat and thin; some plant residue
Hobbs Organic Craft Cotton	100% organically grown and processed cotton Needlepunched with scrim	Up to 6"	Natural color; flat and thin; some plant residue
Fairfield Cotton Classic	80% cotton, 20% polyester Resin bonded	2"–4"	Flat, thin
Hobbs Heirloom Premium Cotton	80% cotton, 20% polyester Needlepunched (no scrim), resin bonded	1/4"–3"	Slight loft; low shrinkage
Double Brushed Cotton Flannelette	100% cotton Napped	Any distance	High quality with adequate thread count—but variable; flat, very thin
Taos Mountain Wool Works Traditional and Designer Light	100% wool Needlepunched	1"–4"	Thin to moderate loft, resilient
Generic Wool (from numerous sources)	100% wool No bonding	1"–4"	Puffy, resilient

Characteristics	Uses	Sizes Available (in inches)
Moderate to low shrinkage; layers stick together; cool in summer; adjusts to body temperature; breathes; cannot be preshrunk	Antique quilt tops, antique quilt reproductions, wall quilts, baby quilts, hot pads, clothing	45 x 60 90 x 108
Can be preshrunk if desired; flatter appearance; can be stiff if over quilted	Wallhangings, throws, bedspreads, craft projects, quilts	45 x 60, 90 x 108, 120 x 120, by the yard, 90 wide
Soft, drapable, stable; can be preshrunk if desired	Quilts, wallhangings, miniatures, garments	36 x 90, 45 x 60, 90 x 108, by the yard, 90 wide
Soft, drapable, stable; can be preshrunk if desired	Quilts, wallhangings, miniatures, garments	36 x 90, 45 x 60, 90 x 108, 120 x 120, by the yard, 90 wide
5%+ shrinkage; layers stick together; cool in summer, warm in winter; adjusts to body temperature; drapable, cuddly; breathes; cannot be preshrunk	Antique quilt tops, antique quilt reproductions, wall quilts, baby quilts, hot pads	81 x 96, 81 x 108
Can be presoaked if desired; can be stiff if over quilted	Wall quilts, crafts, garments	34 x 45, 90 x 108, 120 x 120, by the yard, 90 wide
Soft; stretches; drapes well; good stitch definition; can be preshrunk if desired	Quilts, wallhangings	45 x 60, 90 x 108
Soft drape, pliable; extremely easy to hand quilt; can be preshrunk if desired	Quilts, garments	90 x 108, by the yard, 96 wide
Soft drape, pliable; extremely easy to hand quilt; can be preshrunk if desired	Quilts, crafts, wallhangings	45 x 60, 90 x 108, by the yard, 96 wide
Moderate to low shrinkage; shrinkage allowance should be checked; can be pre soaked if desired; breathes; cool in summer	Quilts, wall quilts, baby quilts, tablecloths, placemats, clothing	45 x 60, 90 x 108
Can be presoaked if desired; extremely easy cotton to hand quilt; durable; drapable; soft; warm	Quilts, baby quilts, wallhangings, garments	45 x 60, 90 x 108, 120 x 120, by the yard, 96 wide
Can shrink to give antique appearance; no loft	Lightweight quilts, baby quilts, lap robes, summer-weight coverlets, tablecloths, placemats, clothing	36 and 45 wide, by the yard
Presoaking not recommended; warm in cold, damp climates; cool in warm weather compared to polyester; resists soiling; recommended to be encased in cheesecloth	Quilts, lap robes, clothing	60 x 90, 80 x 90, 90 x 90, 90 x 108, 90 wide, by the yard
Must be encased in cheesecloth; presoaking not recommended; high resilience; warm in cold, damp climates	Tied comforters, quilts	varies

Brand Name	Fiber Content & Bonding Process	Quilting Distance	Appearance
Hobbs Heirloom Premium Wool	100% wool Resin bonded	1"–3"	Low loft, resilient
Hobbs Poly-Down Polyester	100% polyester Resin bonded	Up to 3"	Extremely soft and resilient; using new generation fibers that are siliconized, moderately thin
Mountain Mist Glazene Process 100% Polyester and Quilt-Light	100% polyester Thermal bonded	$1/8$"–$2 1/2$"	Thin to moderately puffy
Fairfield Low Loft, Extra Loft, High Loft	100% polyester Resin bonded	2"– 4"	Moderate to high loft; various lofts range from $1/4$"–3" thick
Hobbs Thermore	Thermal bonded	Up to 4"	Very thin

LEARNING TO MAKE SMART BATTING CHOICES

Today's quilt battings are made using a variety of fibers, web forming techniques, and finishing techniques. Since each manufacturer uses a different method for producing quilt battings, finding agreement on the "superior" method is unlikely. Therefore, it makes sense for us to investigate how these different fibers and processes affect the finished product, and which batting is best suited to our specific project. I believe there are no "bad" battings, just "misused" battings. But by understanding what batting is about, you will understand how the quilt will look, behave, age, wash, and hang.

Before choosing your next batt, ask yourself these questions:

• Do I want natural, synthetic, or a blended fiber batt?
• Do I want the quilt to be thick or thin?
• Do I want the quilt to be flat or fluffy?
• Do I want to hand or machine quilt it?
• How close do I want to quilt this quilt?
• Do I need this quilt for warmth, or do I want a "cooler" quilt? Is it for summer, spring, fall, or winter temperatures?
• Is the quilt going to be washed a lot or is it just for show?
• Is the quilt going to hang on the wall, or lay on a bed?
• Do I need the quilt to look antique, or contemporary? Should it be smooth or pucker?

If you answer all these questions for every quilt you make, you will be matching the appropriate batting to every quilt top.

Making Batting Samples

To give you an idea of how different battings look, feel, and behave in a quilt, make some samples using different battings. The valuable information you gain by doing this will prevent you from spending time and money on a quilt top that you love, only to be disappointed in

Characteristics	Uses	Sizes Available (in inches)
Soft, drapable; can be presoaked if desired; very warm in cold, damp climates; more comfortable than polyester; very slight bearding if any	Quilts, garments, lap quilts, throws	90 x 108
Warm, very lightweight, very washable, good loft retention	Quilts, throws, lap quilts, pillows	45 x 60, 81 x 96, 90 x 108, 120 x 120
Fibers shift to fill space available; can be quilted extremely close without getting stiff; does not shrink; has look and feel of cotton; heat sensitive	Bed quilts, lap quilts	45 x 60, 72 x 90, 81 x 96, 90 x 108, 120 x 120
Warm, lightweight, heat sensitive; stretches and distorts if hung; low recovery from compression; does not shrink	Bed quilts, lap quilts, pillows, stuffing	45 x 60, 72 x 90, 81 x 96, 90 x 108, 120 x 120
Extremely drapable, easy to quilt, lightweight, does not beard	Garments, miniature quilts, wallhangings, quilts	45 x 54, 90 x 108, by the yard, 90 wide

the final result because the batting appears too flat or too puffy, too stretched or distorted, or simply not right. All you have to do is walk through a quilt show and look at how the quilts hang to know that batting has as much to do with the final look of the quilt as the fabric and pattern do.

With so many different battings on the market and new ones being introduced all the time, it is no wonder quilters are thoroughly confused. If you have ever purchased a new product on the strength of advertising or personal recommendation, then had it perform poorly, you are likely to be gun-shy of trying new products. You have valid concerns. Following is my batting test, which you should approach with an open mind. You will find batting "good guys" and batting "villains." Remember that everyone will have different opinions about which is which, so do your own investigative work.

BATTING TEST

First, collect three to five 14" squares of every batting you can find. If you have trouble obtaining a variety of brands, or getting 14" squares, please contact me at the address on page 135 and I will make the samples available to you. You will need three squares if the batting cannot be preshrunk. You will need five squares if the batting can be preshrunk. Make sure that the brands are labeled so you know which battings you are working with.

Next, make a pile of 14" squares of preshrunk muslin and unwashed muslin (quilt-shop quality only). Label the squares with a permanent marker to identify the prewashed and unwashed. In the center of each of these squares draw a perfect 6" square with a permanent marker.

For the backing squares, sew a 7¼" strip of black cotton to a 7¼" strip of muslin. Cut these strips into 14" squares. You will need a pile of these made from preshrunk and unwashed fabric. Be sure you know which piles are washed and which ones are not.

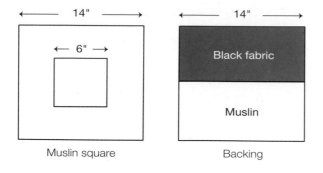

Fabric squares for batting test

You are now ready to layer the batting and fabric together. Do so in the following manner:

• one piece of non-washed batting with non-washed fabric—top and back
• one piece of non-washed batting with pre-washed fabric—top and back
• one piece of prewashed batting with non-washed fabric—top and back
• one piece of prewashed batting with pre-washed fabric—top and back.

Label the muslin square with the brand of batting, whether the batt is prewashed or not, and whether the fabric is prewashed or not.

You should have one square of non-washed batting left. Copy the Sample Sheet on page 122 and staple the remaining batting square to it. Use it as a control sample for future comparison against new batts of the same brand to compare for consistency. If you find that the batting looks and feels different from the one you tested, you may want to run new tests on the new batt to see if it will perform differently than the original.

Now you will need to quilt the samples. If you are a hand quilter, hand quilt the samples. If you hand and machine quilt, do both on each sample. If you only machine quilt, machine quilt your samples. Serge or zigzag around the outside edges. On the form, make a note of whether you enjoyed quilting this batt, and

which method you preferred. Quilt the distances that are within the guidelines on the chart on pages 114-117.

NOTE: I've often been asked what it means when quilting distance is stated as 3" apart or 1" apart. When I asked, I was told that quilting distance was based on channel quilting. You do not have to quilt 3" squares.

This is an excellent time to experiment with various threads and needles. Needles will perform differently in various fibers. One needle may be perfect for polyester, but really drag when going through cotton. The same is true with threads. Just because you have always used one brand of thread with a particular batting doesn't mean a different brand of thread won't work very favorably with a different batting.

Once the squares are quilted, remeasure the 6" square. Using the measurements in the following formula, compute to see if you have lost any size from quilting. This is referred to as *contraction.* Many battings will lose some of their original size simply from the take-up that occurs in the quilting process.

$$\% \text{ shrinkage (or growth)} = \frac{\text{Original length - New length}}{\text{Original length}} \times 100$$

Make a note of any size changes.

Once you have done this, wash and dry the quilt blocks as you would your finished quilts. (Recommended care instructions can be found in Chapter 13.)

Once the blocks are dry, organize them so that all samples from the same brand of batting are together. Look at them and start to form your own opinions. Is one sample too wrinkled and another too flat? Do you really like the sample with the unwashed fabric and the prewashed batting? Or is the sample with the prewashed fabric and unwashed batting better? Start to eliminate the combinations that distort the blocks or just don't appeal to you. You may find you like one combination and your best friend prefers another. This is OK. But remember, you should make quilts that please you, not necessarily everybody else. If you like the final result of one combination—go for it. It's your quilt.

Next, remeasure the 6" square in the center of the block, and rework the shrinkage formulas. This gives you the total amount of size loss due to shrinkage from washing and drying. Now you can use these findings to determine if you need to make your quilt top a bit larger than the finished quilt should be, based on how the batting performs. Shrinkage doesn't need to be feared; learn about it and make it work for you.

The black on the back is to help look for bearding problems. Are tiny fibers migrating through the surface of the fabric? Are lots of fibers migrating? If so, this batt might not be the best choice for dark fabrics. Now look at the top of the block. Is the dark color shadowing through the batting and distorting the color on top? This is a typical problem with polyester battings. The batting is transparent, allowing the color of the backing to shadow through to the top. It also dilutes the color of lights, making them appear slightly gray or tired. Cotton battings are opaque, and light cannot pass through them. Because of this, you will not see color coming through from the back to the top with a cotton batt. The cotton also keeps the true color of the top fabric by providing a "backing" that light cannot penetrate. If you want to put a dark backing on a light quilt top, you can if you are wise about your batting choice.

Once you have filled out the form, wash and dry all the samples again. Continue to do this week after week. Make a mark on each square

every time they are washed and dried. Examine the samples after five washings, again after ten, and so forth. After ten or fifteen washings, see how the batting is holding up. Is this a batting you could use in a baby quilt and wash weekly, if not daily, and have it hold up? Or is it fragile and not aging well under such use? Determine where and when these battings would be appropriate in the quilts you make. Not all quilts lay on closet shelves, but not all quilts are on kids' beds, either.

Determine where and when these battings would be appropriate in the quilts you make. Not all quilts lay on closet shelves, but not all quilts are on kids' beds, either.

OTHER SUGGESTIONS FOR WORKING WITH BATTINGS

Splicing Batting

Battings come in various sizes, but often you need a larger size than is available in a particular brand. This is when you need to splice two batts together to get the needed size. Frequently, two even straight edges are butted and whip-stitched together. However, the problem with this method is that the splice appears as a "break line" through the quilt, with the ridge forming from the whipstitching. Instead of butting two straight edges together, overlap the two pieces of batting by six to eight inches. Cut a serpentine line through both layers. The gradual undulating curves will butt together perfectly once the end of each layer is removed.

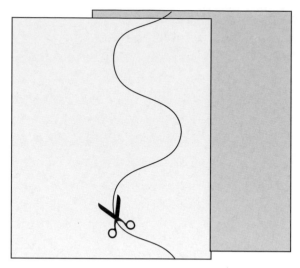

Splicing batting together

Hand stitch the batting together, using about ½"-long, loose herringbone stitches. This serpentine-stitched splice will eliminate any unsightly evidence of where you made the splice.

Herringbone stitch used for joining batting

Batting Grainline

Most battings have a grainline. Some are more prevalent than others. If the fibers were carded or garnetted, there will be an apparent lengthwise grainline. This batting will have little stretch lengthwise, but more noticeable stretch crosswise. If the fibers were air-laid, the fibers will stretch in both directions equally. Needlepunching eliminates much of the stretch. The heavier the needling and denser the fibers, the less stretch there is.

To find the grainline of the batt, gently pull on it from both directions. Like fabric, the length of the batt is stronger and less likely to stretch than the crossgrain. Grain should be considered when layering a quilt, as it will determine which direction you machine quilt first and which direction the quilt should hang on the wall.

When layering a quilt that will be machine quilted using a feeding system, remember that batting grainline is an important consideration. If the quilt is twin, full, or queen-size, the grain of the backing fabric usually runs the length of the quilt. In this case, the grain of the batting also needs to run the length of the quilt. However, for a crib, lap, or king-size quilt, you can save quite a bit of fabric and batting by utilizing the width of the fabric. In this case, the grainline for both the fabric and the batting will go across the width of the quilt. Here, the stretchy grain of the batt goes the length of the quilt. The rule is: Keep the lengthwise grain of the batting with the lengthwise grain of the backing.

I hope that I have accomplished what I set out to do—get you excited about batting and recognize that it is a product that cannot be overlooked or downplayed in the art of quilting.

You need to know this because when you start to quilt, if you quilt the lengthwise seams first, and it is the stretchy, crosswise grain of the batting and backing, you will cause distortion and stretching as you quilt, and the quilt will not lay flat and smooth as a result. If, on the other hand, you always quilt the lengthwise grain seams first, which is the stronger grainline, less stretching and distortion will occur. Then, when you are ready to quilt crosswise, the stretch is contained within the lengthwise seams, and distortion will be minimal.

Another thing you should consider is how the quilt will hang on a wall or at a show. A quilt will hang straighter if the lengthwise grain in both the batting and backing is going the length of the quilt as it hangs on the wall. Gravity can pull and stretch the fabric, and especially the batting, until it sags and distorts terribly. If the stretchy grainline is constantly being pulled by gravity, you can imagine the damage and appearance. On the other hand, the lack of stretch in the lengthwise grain will slow this problem considerably.

I hope that I have accomplished what I set out to do—get you excited about batting and recognize that it is a product that cannot be overlooked or downplayed in the art of quilting. Many of the problems that occur in finished quilts are simply caused by using the wrong batting in that particular quilt. It is not necessarily the batting's fault, but rather a faulty selection process. If you take the time to learn about batting, you will see an instant change in the appearance of your quilts. Confusion is the beginning of knowledge; knowledge is the beginning of comfort and good decision making skills.

BATTING SAMPLE TEST SHEET

Brand name: _____

Fiber content: _____

Sizes available: _____

Recommended quilting distance: _____

How did it needle?

    Hand: _____

    Machine: _____

Thread used:

    Top: _____

    Bobbin: _____

Needle used: _____

Appearance after quilting? _____

Bearding? _____

Shadowing through? _____

Contraction when quilted? _____

Shrinkage after washing? _____

Opinion of appearance after washing:

    Which result did I like best? _____

    Appearance after 5 washings: _____

        after 10 washings: _____

        after 15 washings: _____

Quilts I have used this batting in: _____

Other comments: _____

_____

_____

_____

_____

_____

(See photocopy permission on page 2.)

FROM FIBER TO FABRIC

CHAPTER 13

CARE OF
YOUR QUILTS

CARE AND KEEPING OF FABRICS

After reading the previous text you should be prepared to decide whether or not to pre-wash your fabrics. One thought I would like to leave you with is this: If the fabrics you buy are stored in their new, unwashed state, you are free to make this decision at the time you select them for the project. If they are prewashed before you know what you will do with them, that option is not open to you. Furthermore, unwashed fabrics tend not to fade as fast when exposed to light as prewashed fabrics. And finally, keep in mind that your collection of fabric is more valuable—if you ever wish to sell it—in its unwashed condition.

Storing Fabric

Your sewing room situation is the primary determining factor in how you can store your fabric, and how much you can store.

When I was relegated to a very small workspace, I found I needed to store all my fabrics in boxes, by color. I didn't think much about this until I was able to have a room of my own. When I began taking the fabric out of boxes and putting it on shelves, I could barely contain my excitement. It was indeed a liberating day. The color displayed on the shelves is now a constant source of inspiration and excitement.

If you intend to stack the fabric on shelves, you will need shelves that are 14 inches deep and 32 inches wide between supports. Any deeper and the back part of the shelf is either wasted or inaccessible. If the shelves are wider, they tend to sag.

Michael James suggests that fabric should be stored like books on the shelf, standing upright and supporting each other. This way every fabric is easily accessible and can be pulled from the shelf just as you would a book, instead of digging through piles of fabric that tend to slide and fall over. Measure the folded fabrics and determine the spacing of your shelves if you choose to store your fabric in this manner.

Avoid storing fabric on unfinished wood or particle board shelves, as the acids from the wood can discolor and weaken the fabric. To avoid this problem, paint the wood with a polyurethane finish. Shelves can also be lined with aluminum foil (an inert substance) for further protection.

... keep in mind that your collection of fabric is more valuable—if you ever wish to sell it— in its unwashed condition.

Do not store fabric in plastic bags. Moisture can be trapped inside the bag and lead to mildew. Cotton fabric needs to breathe. You might consider putting glass doors over the fronts of your shelves, or attaching a blind or curtain to the top shelf that can be pulled down when you are not working. These treatments will keep dust and light from your collection.

Clear plastic shoe boxes are wonderful for storing small scraps by color. You can see the colors through the plastic, but the scraps are folded and stacked neatly and ready for use.

For easy reference as to what fabrics are in your collection and how much you have of each, you may want to consider creating reference cards for your fabrics. We do this in our store for inventory purposes, and it could be a great help in controlling a large fabric collection at home. I get very frustrated when trying to work out colors for a quilt and I have to pull out stacks and stacks of fabric to get to the one piece I am looking for on the bottom of the stack. Then, it all has to be put back in order! If you're like me, time is limited, and either I avoid working with the fabric, or it never gets put back properly, leading to frustration the next time out.

This inventory system uses 3 x 5 index cards and a card file drawer. These items are available from the office supply store. Cut a 3" x 5" piece of every fabric in your collection. If you do not want this large a sample, make them the size of your choice. Attach each fabric sample to one index card. On the back of the card make a note of the amount of this fabric that you have, as well as the brand name of the fabric and any other information you can obtain about it from the bolt. This seems like a lot of trouble, but there is good reasoning behind such record keeping. If you need more of the fabric, you can call around to various stores and ask for the fabric by name and number. Without this information the store is looking for a needle in a haystack, based on your description of the fabric. It is likely you will not be very successful. With the computer networks as popular as they are, it is also an excellent way to swap fabric over the wires. You'd be surprised how many quilters know their fabrics by brand name.

Once you have attached all your fabrics to cards, sort them by color, then by value within each color. File them in this order. If you sort your fabrics in this same order on the shelf, you will have no trouble finding them when needed. This is especially helpful if you have to store your fabrics in closed containers. You could develop a numbering system for the containers that gives you immediate access to a particular fabric.

If you do this as soon as you bring the fabric home, it is quite easy and manageable. Instead of prewashing immediately, you take the time you would have spent prewashing becoming organized. The time savings you gain could add

Reference card system used to manage fabric collection

up to the time needed to piece that quilt top!

Along with the other benefits of storing your fabrics in their new (unwashed) state is the fact that it is also the safest method for dye and mildew resistance of the fabric. You will find the fabrics retain their color and vibrancy much longer when stored unwashed.

CARE AND KEEPING OF QUILTS

Once you have learned about fabrics, threads and battings, your purchasing decisions should leave your mind at rest. You will no longer have to fear washing and caring for your finished products. A clean quilt is a healthy quilt! Once your quilts are finished, proper care and storage will ensure years of joy, beauty, and pride. Make a lot of them to use, enjoy, and share.

If you have a quilt that needs laundering, but have not tested the fabrics for colorfastness, you will need to do a spot test before getting the entire quilt wet.

Laundering Your Quilts

I always encounter a lot of anxiety from quilters about washing their quilts, whether they are new or antique. Quilters overlook the fact that soil trapped in the fibers can often cause more damage than the actual laundering process. Textiles are more sensitive to light, airborne dust, pollution, and stains than most other art objects. Consider what the fabric has been exposed to during construction: body oil from your hands, lint from being handled, soil from being on the floor a few times. It's no wonder the quilt is usually quite soiled when it's finished.

Start the cleaning process by vacuuming. This will remove dust particles whose sharp edges start to cut away at the fibers. Buy a two-foot-square piece of fiberglass screening and bind the edges with twill tape. Place the screen on the quilt. Using the corner attachment of the vacuum, gently vacuum over the screen, cleaning the front and back of the quilt.

Sometimes a bath is needed to remove dirt and stains, but washing can permanently damage the quilt if care is not taken. Again, I emphasize pre-testing fabrics for colorfastness at this point. It needs to be done whether you choose to prewash your fabrics or not. Many quilts have bled when they were washed the first time, even though the fabrics were prewashed. This staining is often irreversible. With care, the fabrics used in the quilt can look as fresh and new after the first laundering as they did originally, sometimes even better!

Choose a safe washing agent to clean your quilts. The colorfast testing technique in Chapter 8 will help you determine which detergents are safe. My general guidelines for selecting products are to use those with the least amount of ingredients: something I would be willing to take a bath in. This automatically eliminates general laundry detergents and other washing products that could potentially cause a problem. I highly recommend products such as Orvus Paste, Ultra Ivory dishwashing liquid, and Mountain Mist Ensure. Orvus Paste is packaged under various names and available at quilt shops. I recommend these products because they are neutral and rinse out of the quilt thoroughly.

If you have a quilt that needs laundering, but have not tested the fabrics for colorfastness, you will need to do a spot test before getting the entire quilt wet.

Test any fabric you think might be a problem.

Start by rubbing a dry, white cloth gently over each fabric to see if any color rubs off. If not, go to a blot test. Using a solution of cool water and your favorite quilt cleaning agent, drop a couple of drops of solution onto the color you are testing. Blot with a clean, white cloth. Check for color on the white cotton.

If you find color transference, proceed with caution. It might be advisable to not wet wash the quilt at all. However, if it is truly necessary to clean the quilt, there might be a couple of steps you can take. One is to soak the quilt in *cold* water first. Sometimes this settles the dyestuff and slows or stops the bleeding process. I have had excellent results with a product called Easy Wash®, a soil and stain remover for natural fibers. Easy Wash can take the transferred color out of the fabrics that are stained and clean up the problems. To do this, fill the washer with cold water and add ³/₄ to 1 cup of Easy Wash concentrate. Soak the quilt in this solution for fifteen minutes. (Easy Wash can be applied directly to stained areas as well.) Rinse and check for fading. If the color is gone, proceed to drying. If color is still apparent, repeat the process. Snowy Bleach® is another product that removes excess color when bleeding has occurred. These products are by no means guaranteed to solve the problem, but they do have a good track record.

If the color tests show that the fabrics do not bleed, you can proceed with the washing. (We are discussing the care of new quilts here, not antiques. Consult a textile conservator concerning the care of valuable antique quilts.)

I launder my quilts in the washing machine. The very gentle agitation of my washer has never harmed the quilts. Aggressive agitation can be very damaging. Gentle agitation is not as harmful as the tumbling action of a dryer! Fill the washer to its largest capacity with cool to warm water. Remember, the water should be between 80°F and 85°F for laundering cotton fabrics and quilts. Add the Orvus Paste or your chosen washing agent and agitate to dissolve.

Tip: Orvus Paste can be made into a liquid by mixing it with purified water. I mix a proportion of one tablespoon to a cup of water—one gallon at a time. Then when I need it, I simply pour one cup of the liquid into the washer. I gently lay the quilt in the water and submerge. Then I wash using the gentle cycle, or turn the washer off and let it soak for ten minutes. If you are not using agitation, gently move the quilt in the water with your hands to allow the soil to release from the fabric. Do this for about five minutes. Detergent has the ability to clean for only twelve to fifteen minutes. If the water is very soiled, you will need to repeat this process until the quilt appears clean. (Soaking in the same dirty water for a long period of time will not get the quilt clean.)

Spinning will not harm the quilt, and is much easier on the fibers than handling a heavy, dripping-wet quilt.

Spin the water out of the quilt on the gentle spin cycle. Spinning will not harm the quilt, and is much easier on the fibers than handling a heavy, dripping-wet quilt. Note: This method is not recommended for king-size quilts. Extra large, front loading washers are recommended for laundering any large spread or quilt.

To rinse, carefully remove the quilt from the washer and fill the tub with cool water. Keep the water temperature for washing and rinsing the same. Place the quilt in the water and gently move it around to remove the washing agent from the fibers. Drain the water and spin. If possible, watch as the water drains from the tub. If soapy residue continues to come from the water, rinse again. The water should run completely clear at the end of the cycle to indicate that the quilt is thoroughly rinsed. This may take as many as five rinsings, depending on the washing agent and amount of detergent used.

There are differing opinions as to how to dry a quilt, but do not put a wet quilt in the clothes dryer! The tumbling action is hard on the quilt. It can also cause crocking (the loss of surface color by friction) and streaking of the fabric colors. I think the best way to dry a quilt is to lay it flat. There are many ways to dry quilts flat. Drying quilts outdoors on a dry, breezy, sunny day is fast and easy. I use two sheets—one on the ground and one on top of the quilt—to protect the quilt from insects and the sun. Grommets can be put in the corners of the

---

There are differing opinions as to how to dry a quilt, but do not put a wet quilt in the clothes dryer.

---

sheets so they can be staked down to prevent blowing in the breeze. When the top is dry to the touch, turn it over to dry the back side. I have also had success drying quilts over large bushes. Cover the bush with a sheet, lay the quilt over the bush, and cover with another sheet. The bush allows the quilt to be off the ground, yet provides total support and air circulation.

If you need to dry indoors, lay the quilt on a floor, bed, or over the sofa, using sheeting or plastic to protect the surface you are laying the quilt on. Oscillating and/or ceiling fans will speed the drying process considerably. Creating a large drying screen from a piece of mosquito netting, fiberglass screen, etc., can also be helpful in getting the quilt off the floor and aiding air circulation. Never hang a wet quilt because the stress of hanging can weaken the fabrics and tear the stitches. When the quilt is barely damp dry, you can fluff the quilt a bit by placing it in the dryer on air or fluff—no heat.

Guidelines for the Care of Wool Quilts

Today's wool battings are made to be washable without undue shrinkage. With proper care, quilts with wool batting will endure much longer than those with polyester.

Be very careful when choosing a washing agent for wool quilts. An alkaline detergent can cause wool fibers to shrink even in cool water. You will want to use a neutral, non-ionic detergent that does not contain enzymes, fabric brighteners, or whiteners. Orvus Paste and Ultra Ivory dishwashing liquid are perfect choices for wool quilts, as well as any detergent recommended by the American Wool Council.

Wash wool quilts in cool to lukewarm water (no warmer than 85°F). A cold water wash and rinse is best for the wool, but if the quilt is soiled, warm water will assist the cleaning process. It is very important to keep the wash and rinse water temperatures as close to one another as possible.

The ideal way to wash a wool quilt is by hand. Agitation should be minimal, if done at all, and only on the gentle cycle. Wash for thirty to forty-five seconds, then let the quilt soak for four to five minutes, followed by about one minute of light agitation. Rinse by gently agitating for thirty to forty-five seconds, then spin the water out. Repeat if necessary. The more agitation the quilt is put through, the more shrinkage (felting) is possible for the batt. Spinning does not damage the wool in any way, so it is preferable to spin on gentle to remove excess water after washing and rinsing. This also reduces drying time.

If at all possible, lay the quilt flat to dry. The dryer causes excessive agitation, and the uneven heat causes shrinkage (felting). If you must dry in the dryer, do it on the lowest heat setting. If possible dry the quilt flat until just damp, then tumble for a few minutes to fluff and soften the fabric.

Keep your wool quilts clean. Heavy soiling is not only hard on the fabrics, but vigorous washing to remove heavy soiling is harder on the wool than more frequent launderings.

Finally, the more the wool is quilted, the more the quilt is stabilized and the less chance there is of any shrinkage. On the other hand, if quilted too closely, the air space within the fibers is flattened and the warmth will be less.

On page 133 I have provided care labels that can be photocopied onto fabric and sewn onto the back of your quilts. Feel free to also write your own instructions. For the future health and safekeeping of your quilt, I highly recommend adding care labels.

Storing Quilts

When not in use, quilts should be stored carefully. We tend to think that only old or antique quilts need special care and consideration. However, if new quilts are to remain beautiful and damage-free in the years to come, you need to consider how they are cared for today. Quilts are ideally stored unfolded, flat, and unstacked. However, few of us have the luxury of this kind of space.

Avoid storing quilts or any textiles, in attics or basements. Attics are too hot and basements are too damp. Ideal storage temperatures are between 60°F and 70°F. Humidity levels need to be between forty-five and sixty percent. Humidity is the real killer for quilts—it causes mold and mildew problems. Quilts should be stored within the living area of your home, preferably away from outside walls, in an area with air circulation that is dark most of the time. A good guideline is that if the temperature and humidity level are comfortable to you, it will also be good for your quilts.

Avoid using plastic bags. Plastic cuts off air circulation and emits harmful by-products as it ages. The static electricity generated by plastics attracts dust, which is also undesirable. Finally, mold and mildew result from moisture trapped inside plastic bags. If you see little black spots on a quilt, which indicate mildew, very little can be done. (See Quilt Restoration Society in Sources on page 135.) (Mildew can also be detected by the odor.) Prevent mildew with good air circulation.

Use well-washed and rinsed cotton muslin sheeting and no fabric softeners or dryer sheets, or acid-free tissue paper to protect quilts from wood surfaces, dust, light, and abrasion. Fabric wrappings can be washed once a year; tissue paper needs to be changed at least that often.

Folded Storage

Storing a folded quilt presents a major problem: Fold lines create stress on the quilted fabric, stitches, and batting. You can reduce this stress by padding the folded areas with tissue paper or cotton sheeting. Lay the quilt out on a clean, flat surface. Place a sheet of acid-free tissue paper on the center of the quilt. Make a crumpled roll and place it across the quilt so that the top third of the quilt can be folded over the roll. Place another roll of paper across the lower third of the quilt, and fold the lower third over the roll. Now the quilt is folded in thirds. Place a shorter roll of paper across the folded quilt a third of the way in. Fold the left side toward the center. Repeat with the right side. Avoid stacking quilts if possible, as this counteracts the tissue paper padding.

Once the quilt has been folded, it is ready for storage. Acid-free boxes are a good choice if your space is limited and you need to stack the quilts. A box keeps stress off the quilt directly, but it does reduce air circulation.

If you need to store your quilts in a blanket chest, be very careful that the fabric does not come into direct contact with the wood, especially if the wood is unsealed, like cedar. Wood gives off detrimental acids, and you will need several layers of protective material between the wood and fabric. Wrap your quilt in well-washed and rinsed cotton sheeting before storing near a wood surface. If the quilt will be on a shelf, put several coats of polyurethane on the wood before placing the quilt on it. Even then, line the shelves with acid-free tissue paper.

Quilts stored in this manner need to be refolded frequently to avoid permanent creasing, a tear, or any other wear mark. Fold a different direction each time, in halves, thirds, or in triangles like a flag.

Rolled Storage

There is some controversy over whether or not a quilt should be rolled. Some conservators say that only a single-layer textile should be rolled, while others say that quilts can benefit from this technique. If you have the space, your quilts can be rolled around a large tube that measures at least three inches in diameter. It should be longer than the width of the quilt. Roll the quilt loosely, with no wrinkles, and with the top to the inside if it is a pieced quilt. This puts minimum stress on the stitches. Cover the tube with cotton fabric or acid-free

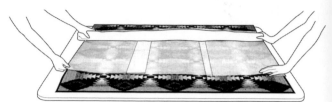

Tissue roll for top third of quilt

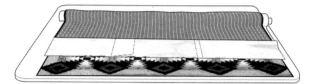

Top third folded over roll

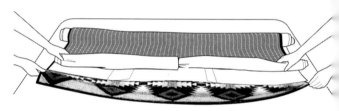

Tissue roll for bottom third

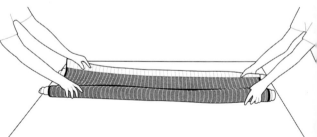

Bottom third folded over roll

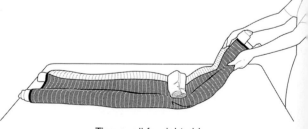

Tissue roll for right side

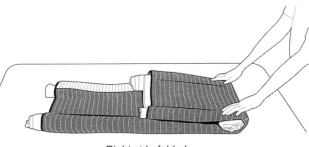

Right side folded

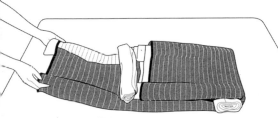

Tissue roll for left side

Left side folded

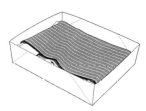

Stored in acid-free box

tissue paper. (The cover will need to be renewed once a year.) Once the quilt is rolled, cover it with a clean cotton sheet. The tubes, if strong enough, can be stored on wall brackets in a dark, clean, well-ventilated area. If the tube is too weak, run a strong rod through it.

All quilts need to spend some time opened out and on their backs. Quilt curators suggest airing them every six months, or at least once a year. Lay them on the floor or on a bed for several days. On a dry, warm day, lay them between two sheets on the grass to air for three or four hours. This will give you a chance to wash their coverings to remove dust and wood acids that may have been absorbed.

Once a quilt is stored, don't forget about it for long periods of time. Even with careful storage, pests can cause problems. At least once a year the quilt needs to be refolded and have its wrapping washed or replaced. While doing this, carefully vacuum the quilt surfaces to remove moth eggs, dust particles, etc. Moth crystals in the vacuum bag will kill any insects sucked up in the cleaning process so they can't escape.

If you have problems with moths in wool or wool-filled quilts, there are several solutions. One is to dry-clean the item. You can also try freezing the quilt for about two months, or vacuuming, then treating with moth balls (paradichlorobenzene, PDCB.) Do not use naphthalene moth balls. One method given in *The Quilt Digest* by Michael Kile is to use two garbage bags, one inside the other. Loosely fold the quilt and place it in the bags. Put a lot of PDCB moth balls in a cotton cloth, twist, and tie at the top. Make sure this bag of moth balls sits on top of the quilt. Tightly seal the bag and leave it for at least a week, possibly two. The warmer the temperature (preferably around seventy degrees), the better this treatment will work. Mothballs are a good general treatment for all insects.

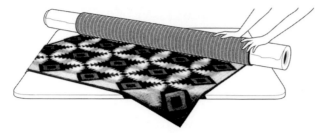

Roll quilt loosely onto a covered tube.

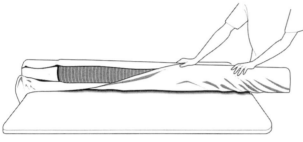

Cover rolled quilt with muslin.

If you feel you need to treat an area for insects, suspend a cloth bag of moth balls from the ceiling in your storage closet. The fumes are heavier than air, so the bag needs to be placed above the items you want to treat. Use a heavy concentration of PDCB for two months, rather than a small amount continuously. Do not allow the chemical to come into direct contact with the fabric.

Avoid having your best quilts around smokers. Cigarette smoke soaks into fabric faster and deeper than anything. Smoke can cause color changes and it also speeds the deterioration of the fibers in the quilt.

Because quilts are an art form and are valuable not only in dollars, but in their sentimental value, they deserve special attention. A new quilt, as well as one made many years ago, can be ruined by improper storage, display, use, and cleaning. Treat quilts with care, and they will bring you joy for many, many years.

SUMMARY

I sincerely hope that you have enjoyed the adventure that this book has led you through. If you took the time to work through the testing procedures of fabrics and battings, you surely have a much higher awareness and comfort level for the textiles that we use in quiltmaking. This book was written to be reference manual for you. I certainly don't expect anyone to absorb all this information at one time. If you encounter a problem with a fabric in your quilt, refer back to Chapter 8 and retrace your steps in caring for the fabric and see if you can identify what might have been missed. If you are deciding on a batting for your next quilt, be sure to refer to the list of questions on page 116 before making a final decision. If you are having trouble with the stitch quality from your machine, refer to Chapters 10 and 11 to see if your thread is causing you problems.

A reference like this has never been made available to quilters, and I hope that it has a powerful and positive impact on the textiles that you work with as well as the finished products derived from them.

Care of Your Heirloom Quilt
100% cotton top and back
100% cotton batting

For best results:
• Fill washer with 80°F-85°F water. Treat water if a chlorine odor is present. Thoroughly dissolve 1 Tbsp. Orvus Paste or ¼ cup Ultra Ivory dishwashing liquid in the water. Gently agitate quilt in water for 15 minutes. If heavily soiled, drain water and repeat. • Spin to remove soapy water. • Remove quilt and fill washer with 80°F-85°F water again. Treat for chlorine again if necessary. Rinse by agitating very gently. • Spin to remove water. • Lay out on clean sheet and block to dry. Can be fluffed in warm dryer when just damp. • Store in fabric bag and keep away from light. Refold often.

Care of Your Heirloom Quilt
100% cotton top and back
100% polyester batting

For best results:
Fill washer with 80°F-85°F water. Treat water if a chlorine odor is present. Thoroughly dissolve 1 Tbsp. Orvus Paste or ¼ cup Ultra Ivory dishwashing liquid in the water. Gently agitate quilt in water for fifteen minutes. If heavily soiled, drain water and repeat. • Spin to remove soapy water. • Remove quilt and fill washer with 80°F-85°F water again. Treat for chlorine again if necessary. Rinse by agitating very gently. • Spin to remove water. Dry in permanent press setting dryer. Remove quilt from dryer just before quilt is completely dry; lay flat to finish drying. • Store in fabric bag and keep away from light. Refold often.

Care of Your Heirloom Quilt
100% cotton top and back
100% wool batting

For best results:
Fill washer with 80°F-85°F water. Treat water if a chlorine odor is present. Thoroughly dissolve 1 Tbsp. Orvus Paste or ¼ cup Ultra Ivory dishwashing liquid in the water. Gently agitate quilt in water for 15 minutes. If heavily soiled, drain water and repeat. Spin to remove soapy water. • Remove quilt and fill washer with 80°F-85°F water again. Treat for chlorine again if necessary. Rinse by agitating very gently. • Spin to remove water. Lay out and block on a clean sheet to dry. Can fluff in cool dryer when barely damp. • Store in fabric bag and keep away from light. Refold often.

Care of Your Heirloom Quilt
100% cotton top and back
80% cotton, 20% polyester batting

For best results:
Fill washer with 80°F-85°F water. Treat water if a chlorine odor is present. Thoroughly dissolve 1 Tbsp. Orvus Paste or ¼ cup Ultra Ivory dishwashing liquid in the water. Gently agitate quilt in water for 15 minutes. If heavily soiled, drain water and repeat. • Spin to remove soapy water. • Remove quilt and fill washer with 80°F-85°F water again. Treat for chlorine again if necessary. Rinse by agitating very gently. • Spin to remove water. • Either lay out and block to dry or dry in permanent press setting dryer. • Remove quilt from dryer just before quilt is completely dry; lay flat to finish drying. • Store in fabric bag and keep away from light. Refold often.

(See photocopy permission on page 2.)

APPENDIX I

Listed here are the current major manufacturers and converters of today's quilting cottons. I have included this list for your information, and to make it easy for you to contact these companies if you need to ask about your test findings as they pertain to their product.

Benartex, Inc.
1460 Broadway, 8th Floor
New York, NY 10036
212/840-3250

Concord House
1359 Broadway
New York, NY 10018
212/760-0300

Dan River Inc.
1325 Avenue of the Americas
New York, NY 10019
212/554-5662

Fabri-Quilt, Inc.
901 East 14th Avenue
North Kansas City, MO 64116
816/421-2000

Fabric Traditions
1350 Broadway, Suite 2106
New York, NY 10018
212/279-5710

Fasco/Fabric Sales, Inc.
6250 Stanley Avenue South
Seattle, WA 98108
800/874-0541

Hoffman California/International
    Fabrics
25792 Obrero Drive
Mission Viejo, CA 92691
800/457-0100

Indo-US Sales, Inc.
164 North Brandon Drive
P.O. Box 5114
Glendale Heights, IL 60139
708/893-8536

John Kaldor Fabricmaker USA, LTD.
500 Seventh Street
New York, NY 10018
212/221-8270

Robert Kaufman Co., Inc.
129 West 132nd Street
Los Angeles, CA 90061
800/877-2066

Kona Bay Fabrics
3043 Lopeka Place
Honolulu, HI 96817
808/595-0660

Libas Limited
1333 South Hope Street
Los Angeles, CA 90015
213/747-2406

Liberty of London Prints, Ltd.
313 Merton Road
London, England SW18 5JS

Marcus Brothers Textiles
1460 Broadway
New York, NY 10036
212/354-8700

Moda Fabrics
13795 Hutton
Dallas, TX 75234
214/484-8901

Momen House
1840 West 205th Street
Torrance, CA 90501
310/787-0086

Northcott/Monarch
229 West 36th Street
New York, NY 10018
212/563-0450

P & B Textiles
1580 Gilbreth Road
Burlingame, CA 94010
415/692-0422

Peter Pan Fabrics/Henry Glass & Co.
1071 Sixth Avenue
New York, NY 10018
212/840-8200

RJR Fashion Fabric
13748 South Gramercy Place
Gardena, CA 90249
800/422-5426

Spectrix Fabrics
20-21 Wagaraw Road
Fairlawn, NJ 07410
201/423-5525

Speigel Fabrics
6464 Flotilla Street
Commerce, CA 90040
213/888-1651

Springmaid Fabrics
Wamsutta/OTC Div. of Springs
    Industries
104 West 40th Street
New York, NY 10018
212/556-6500

APPENDIX II

Listed below are the current major manufacturers of quilt battings. This list is included for your information and to make it easy for you to contact these companies if need be.

Air-Lite Synthetics Mfg. Inc.
342 Irwin Street
Pontiac, MI 48341-2982
810/335-8131

Fairfield Processing Corp.
88 Rose Hill Avenue
Danbury, CT 06810
203/744-2090

Hobbs Bonded Fibers
P.O. Box 2521
Waco, TX 76702
800/433-3357

Morning Glory Products
Division of Carpenter Co.
302 Highland Drive
Taylor, TX 76574
512/352-6311

Mountain Mist
The Stearns Technical Textiles Co.
100 Williams Street
Cincinnati, OH 45215-4683
513/948-5276

Kelsul, Inc.
Quilters Cotton Batting
3205 Foxgrove Lane
Chesapeake, VA 23321
804/484-7611

Warm Products, Inc.
16110 Woodinville-Redmond Road, #4
Woodinville, WA 89072
206/488-4464

SOURCES

Quilt Restoration Society
P.O. Box 337
Hillsdale, NY 12529
518/325-4502
518/325-6625 fax

Harriet's Treadle Arts
6390 West 44th Avenue
Wheatridge, CO 80033
303/424-1290

GLOSSARY OF TEXTILE TERMS

abrasion: the wearing away of any part of a material from rubbing against another surface.

absorbency: the ability of one material to take up another material.

affinity: a chemical attraction; the tendency of two elements or substances to unite or combine, such as fiber and dyestuff.

afterglow: the glow that remains after the disappearance of a flame; afterglow follows cessation of the combustion of certain solid materials.

alkaline: a term used to describe a material having a pH greater than 7.0 in water.

antichlor: a chemical, such as sodium thiosulfate, used to remove excess chlorine.

bale: a large bundle prepared for shipping, storage, or sale; especially a standardized quantity of goods, such as ginned cotton, that is compressed, bound, and sometimes wrapped.

batting: a soft bulky assemblage of fibers, usually carded. Batting is sold in sheets or rolls and is used especially for quilts, comforter stuffings, and other thermal applications, or for stuffing or packaging.

beam: a wood or metal cylinder, usually with a circular flange on each end, on which warp yarns are wound for dyeing, weaving, or warp knitting.

bearding: fuzz on the surface of an item resulting from loose fibers migrating through to the surface of a fabric.

binder fibers: fibers which can act as an adhesive in a web because their melting point is relatively low compared with that of the other fibers in the material.

bleaching: any of several processes to remove the natural and artificial impurities in fabrics to obtain clear whites for finished fabric or in preparation for dyeing and finishing.

bleeding: loss of color by a fabric or yarn when immersed in water, a solvent, or similar liquid medium, as a result of improper dyeing, the use of poor quality dyes, or the chemical reaction between the dye and liquid solution in which the fabric is immersed, such as chlorine in water. Fabrics that bleed can cause staining of white or light-colored fabrics when in contact with them while wet.

bonding: a process of binding fibers into a nonwoven fabric (batting) using mechanical, chemical, or thermal means.

bowed fabric: when the filling yarns curve and do not go straight across the fabric. It is generally caused by improper tenter frame procedures. On-grain fabric should have less than a $^{3}/_{8}$" variance in 45"-wide fabric.

broadcloth: a tightly woven, lustrous cotton or cotton/polyester blend fabric in a plain weave with a crosswise rib. It resembles poplin, but the rib is finer.

calender: a machine used in finishing to impart a variety of surface effects to fabrics. It consists of two or more heavy rollers, sometimes heated, through which the fabric passes under heavy pressure.

calendering: a mechanical finishing process for fabrics to produce surface effects, such as high luster, glazing, moiré, and embossed effects. The fabric is passed between heavy, heated rolls under pressure.

calico: a lightweight, plain woven, inexpensive fabric, usually cotton, characteristically having small figured designs on a contrasting background.

card: a machine used in the manufacture of staple yarns. Its functions are to separate, align, and deliver the fibers in a sliver form and to remove impurities.

carding: a process in the manufacture of spun yarns whereby the staple is opened, cleaned, aligned, and formed into a continuous, untwisted strand called a sliver.

cellulose: a carbohydrate which is the chief component of the cell walls of plants. Cellulose is found in wood and

in cotton, linen, jute, hemp, and all the bast, leaf, and stem fibers. It is a basic raw material in the manufacture of rayon, acetate, and triacetate fibers.

chintz: a light to medium-weight, plain-woven fabric with a glazed (polished) finish produced by friction calendering.

color change: any change in the lightness, hue, and/or saturation of a treated color compared to the corresponding untreated color.

colorant: a material, such as dye or pigment, used to give color to something.

colorfastness: the resistance of a material to change any of its color characteristics and/or to transfer its colorant(s) to adjacent materials. Loss of color can occur during processing, testing, storage, and use of a material; it can result from the type of dye used, improper dyeing procedures, light, detergents, chlorine, etc.

combing: a process subsequent to carding in cotton and worsted system processing which straightens the fibers and extracts neps, foreign matter, and short fibers. Combing produces a stronger, more even, more compact, finer, smoother yarn.

converter: an individual or organization which buys greige fabrics and sells them as a finished product to cutters, wholesalers, retailers, and others. The converter arranges for the finishing of the fabric, namely bleaching, mercerizing, dyeing, printing, etc., to the buyer's specifications.

cotton fiber: a natural fiber composed of almost pure cellulose. As taken from plants, the fiber is found in lengths of $^{3}/_{8}$ to 2 inches.

crease-resistant finish: a term used to describe a fabric chemically treated to improve its resistance to and recovery from wrinkling.

crocking: the rubbing off of dye from a fabric as a result of insufficient dye penetration or fixation, the use improper dyes or dyeing methods, and/or insufficient washing and treatment after the dyeing operation. Crocking can occur under wet or dry conditions.

crystalline: consisting or made of crystals. The degree of crystallinity influences the physical properties of fibers.

denier: a unit of weight for measuring the fineness of thread. Denier is equivalent numerically to the number of grams per 9,000 meters in which the lower numbers represent the finer sizes and the higher numbers the coarser sizes.

detergent: a synthetic cleaning agent containing surfactants that do not precipitate in hard water and have the ability to emulsify oil and suspend dirt.

doctor blade: a metal knife which cleans or scrapes the excess dye from engraved printing rollers, leaving dye paste only in the engraved areas.

drawing: the process of increasing the length per unit weight of laps, slivers, slubbings, or rovings.

dyeing: a process of coloring fibers, yarn, fabrics, or finished goods with either natural or synthetic dyes.
1. beam dyeing: a high temperature dyeing process in which warp yarns or fabrics are wound onto a special beam, the barrel of which is evenly perforated with holes. The dye liquor is forced through the yarn or fabric from the inside out and from the outside in.
2. pad dyeing: a process of passing the fabric through a trough containing dye, then squeezing it between to heavy rollers or pads to remove excess dye.
3. piece dyeing: dyeing fabrics "in the piece," i.e., in fabric form after weaving as opposed to yarn or stock form.
4: skein dyeing: dyeing yarn in the form of skeins or hanks.
5. stock dyeing: dyeing fibers in staple form.
6. yarn dyeing (package): dyeing yarn before the fabric is woven or knit.

dye range: a broad term referring to the collection of dye and chemical baths, drying equipment, etc. in a continuous-dyeing line.

dyes: substances which add color to textiles by absorption into the fiber.
1. direct dyes: a class of dyestuffs which are applied directly to the substrate in a neutral or alkaline bath. They give bright shades but exhibit poor washfastness.
2. fiber-reactive dyes: a type of water soluble anionic dye having affinity for cellulose fibers, used when bright shades are desired.
3. Napthol (azoic) dyes: a type of compound formed on the fiber by first treating the fiber with a phenolic compound. The fiber is then immersed in a second solution containing a diazonium salt which reacts with the phenolic compound to produce a colored azo compound. Used mainly for cellulose fibers. Produces brilliant shades at a relatively low cost.
4. sulfur dyes: a class of synthetic dyes based on sulfur. Used mainly on cottons for economical dark shades with moderate to good fastness to washing and light. They generally have poor fastness to chlorine.
5. vat dyes: a commercial class of dyes, among the most resistant to washing and sunlight. Widely used in cellulosic fibers; limited use with wool and silk because of the alkaline bath which has a deteriorating effect on animal fibers.

end: a warp yarn which runs vertically in a woven fabric.

fabric: a textile structure produced by interlacing yarns, fibers, or filaments.

fastness: the ability of a dye to retain its color when exposed to conditions or agents such as light, perspiration, atmospheric gases, or washing that can remove or destroy the color. A dye may be reasonably fast to one agent and only moderately fast to another.

fiber: the basic unit used in the fabrication of textile yarn and fabrics.

filament: a fiber of indefinite or extreme length such as found naturally in silk. Man-made filaments are extruded into filaments which are converted into filament yarn.

filling: the yarn running crosswise, from selvage to selvage, at right angles to the warp. Each crosswise length is called a pick.

finish: a mechanical or chemical process applied to textile materials to produce a desired surface effect. Finishes are classified as permanent, durable, semi-durable, or temporary.

fixation: the process of setting a dye after dyeing or printing, usually by steaming or other heat treatment.

flame resistant: a term used to describe a material that burns slowly or is self-extinguishing after removal of an external source of ignition.

flame retardant: a chemical compound applied during manufacture or processing of a fiber, fabric, or other textile item to reduce its flammability.

formaldehyde: a colorless, pungent gas used primarily as a disinfectant and preservative, and in the manufacture of synthetic resins, dyes, etc.

frosting: a change in fabric color caused by localized, abrasive wear.

garnetting: a process for reducing various textile waste materials to fiber by passing them through a machine called a garnett, which is similar to a card.

gray scale: a scale of gray chips representing progressive differences in color or contrast corresponding to numerical colorfastness ratings.

greige goods: a fabric just off the loom in an unfinished state.

hand: the tactile qualities of a fabric perceived by touch, e.g., softness, firmness, elasticity, drapability, fineness, resilience, etc.

jig: a machine in which fabric in open-width form is transferred repeatedly from one roller to another, passing each time through a relatively small bath. Jigs are used for scouring, dyeing, bleaching, and finishing.

lightfastness: the degree of resistance of dyed textile materials to the color-destroying influence of light, especially sunlight.

linters: the short cotton fibers which adhere to the seed during the first ginning.

long staple: a long fiber; in reference to cotton, long staple indicates a fiber length of not less than 1 1/8 inches.

machine twist: a hard-twist sewing thread, usually 3-ply, spun with S-twist and plied with Z-twist, made especially for use in sewing machines.

mercerization: a treatment of cotton yarn or fabric to increase its luster and affinity for dyes. The process causes a permanent swelling of the fiber and thus increases its luster.

migration: the movement of dye from one area of dyed fabric to another. This includes movement of color from a dyed area to an undyed area of cloth and from one fabric to another fabric in the same wash water.

monofilament: any single filament of a man-made fiber.

mordant: a chemical used on some textile fibers to increase their affinity for dyes.

nap: a fuzzy or downy surface given to a cloth when part of the fiber is raised from the basic structure.

napping: a finishing process that raises the surface fibers of a fabric by means of passing rapidly revolving cylinders covered with metal points over the fabric.

needlepunching: the process of converting batts or webs of loose fibers into a coherent nonwoven fabric on a needle loom. When the barbed needles are forced (punched) through the thick web of fibers, enough fibers are entangled to constitute a nonwoven fabric.

nonionic: not dependent on a surface-active (surfactant) anion for effect.

nonwoven fabric: an assembly of textile fibers held together by mechanical interlocking in a random web or mat, by fusing the fibers with heat, or by bonding with a cementing medium such as starch, glue, latex, etc.

pick: a single filling thread carried by one trip of the weft insertion device across the loom.

pigment: an insoluble, finely divided substance used to deluster or color fibers, yarns, or fabrics.

pill: a small accumulation of fibers on the surface of a fabric that become entangled in a tiny ball. Pilling can develop during wear when abrasion or friction is applied.

plain weave: the most basic and common weave used in woven fabric whereby each filling yarn passes successively over and under each warp yarn, alternating each row.

ply: the number of single yarns twisted together to form a plied yarn, or the number of plied yarns twisted together to form cord.

plying: twisting together two or more single yarns or ply yarns to form, ply yarn or cord, respectively.

print: a fabric with designs applied by means of engraved rollers, blocks, or screens using dyes or pigments.

print paste: the mixture of gum or thickener, dye, and appropriate chemicals used in printing fabrics. Viscosity varies according to the type of printing equipment, type of cloth, degree of penetration desired, etc.

printing: the process of producing a pattern on yarns, warp, or fabric. The color or other treating material, usually in the form of a paste, is deposited onto the fabric and is then usually treated with steam, heat, or chemicals for fixation.
1. direct printing: a process in which the colors for the desired designs are applied directly to the white or dyed cloth.
2. discharge printing: a process in which the fabric is piece dyed, then printed with a paste containing a chemical which removes the color where the designs are desired. Sometimes a color is added to the discharge paste in order to replace the discharged color with another shade.
3. pigment printing: a printing method in which pigments are used instead of dyes. The pigments do not penetrate the fiber but are affixed to the surface of the fabric by means of synthetic resins (binders) which are cured after application to make them insoluble. The colors produced are bright and generally colorfast, but crocking can occur.
4. resist printing: a printing method in which the design is produced by applying a resist agent (and sometimes a dye) in the desired design, then dyeing the fabric. When the resist material is washed out or removed, the design remains.

5. roller printing: the application of designs to fabric, using a machine containing a series of engraved metal rollers positioned around a large padded cylinder. Print paste is fed to the rollers and a doctor blade scrapes the paste from the unengraved portion of the roller. Each roller applies one color to the finished design.
6. screen printing: a method of printing similar to using a stencil. The areas of the screen through which the coloring matter is not to pass are filled with a waterproof material. The print paste which contains the dye is then forced through the untreated portions of the screen onto the fabric below.

registration: aligning rollers, screens, and stencils so that each part of the design fits into the designated area and does not overlap or leave open spaces.

relaxation shrinkage: the contraction of a fiber, yarn, or fabric resulting from the relief of tension created during processing.

repeat: the distance covered by a single unit of a pattern that is duplicated over and over, measured along the length of the fabric.

residual shrinkage: the amount of shrinkage remaining in a fabric after finishing, expressed as a percentage of the dimensions before finishing.

resin: a general term for solid or semi-solid natural organic substances, usually of vegetable origin and amorphous and yellowish to brown, transparent or translucent, and soluble in alcohol or ether but not in water, or any of a large number of man-made products to have the same properties of natural resins.

ring-spinning: a system of spinning using a ring and traveler take-up in which the drawing of the roving, and the twisting and winding of the yarn onto the bobbin proceed simultaneously and continuously.

rotor-spinning: a system of spinning based on the concept of introducing twist into the yarn without package rotation, by simply rotating the yarn end at a gap or break in the flow of the fibers between the delivery system and the yarn package.

roving: a loose assemblage of fibers drawn into a single strand, with very little twist; an intermediate state between sliver and yarn. Roving is a condensed sliver which has been drawn, twisted, doubled, and redoubled.

satin weave: one of three basic weaves, characterized by warp yarns floating over a predetermined number of filling yarns, e.g. sateens.

scouring: a finishing process to remove dirt, sizing, and oil from fabric prior to dyeing.

screen: a stencil used in screen printing, made of fine silk, metal, nylon, or polyester filaments. The screen is perforated in specific areas to form a design and then mounted on a frame. The paste containing the dye is forced through the perforations onto the fabric, leaving the design. A series of screens, one for each color, is used for multicolored designs.

scrim: a lightweight, nonwoven fabric that is placed on top of a crosslapped fiber web before it is needlepunched. Provides stability to the fiber web.

selvages: the closely-woven, finished edges running parallel to the warp that prevent the cloth from raveling.

shrinkage: contraction in length and/or width of a material caused by fabric design, construction, yarn twist, and finishing. Shrinkage occurs especially during washing and drying.

singeing: a finishing process which removes protruding fibers from yarn or fabric by passing it over a flame or heated copper plates. Singeing gives fabric a smooth surface and is necessary for fabrics which are to be printed.

skewed fabric: a fabric whose filling yarns are straight, but do not run perpendicular to the fabric edges (selvages).

sliver: a continuous strand of loosely assembled fibers without twist. The sliver is carded, (possibly combed), and drawn, before it is eventually twisted into a spun yarn.

soap: a cleansing agent produced by the reaction of a caustic soda and a fat.

spinneret: a metal disc containing numerous minute holes used in yarn extrusion. The spinning solution or melted polymer is forced through the holes to form the yarn filaments.

spinning: the processes used to make single yarns from fiber.

spinning frame: a machine used for spinning staple yarn. It draws the roving to the desired size, inserts twist, and winds the yarn onto a bobbin.

squeegee: the portion of a screen-printing apparatus consisting of a blade which forces the print paste through the screen onto the fabric.

staining: the unintended transference of colorant to a fabric from contact with a dyed or pigmented material.

staple: natural fibers or cut lengths from filaments.

tailing: when individual colors separate out of solution causing unevenness of color.

tensile strength: the ability of a fiber, yarn, or fabric to resist breaking under tension, expressed in pounds per inch.

tenter frame: a machine that finishes fabric to a specified width under tension. The fabric is held firmly at the edges by pins or clips to a pair of continuous chains on horizontal tracks. As the fabric advances through the heated chamber, it is adjusted to the desired width.

textile: a fabric which has been woven, knitted, felted, bonded, braided, crocheted, or knotted.

thermoplastic: a term used to describe a plastic material which is permanently fusible. The term applied to true man-made fibers describes their tendency to soften at higher temperatures.

thread: a tightly-twisted, special type of yarn, usually ply, used for sewing. Made of cotton, silk, rayon, nylon, and polyester, etc.

thread count: the number of ends (warp yarns) and picks (filling yarns) per linear inch in a woven cloth.

transference: the movement of a chemical, dye, or pigment between fibers within a fabric or between fabrics.

traveler: a C-shaped, metal clip which revolves around the ring on a ring spinning frame. It guides the yarn onto the bobbin as twist is inserted into the yarn.

twist: the number of turns per unit length about the axis of a fiber, roving, yarn, or cord. *See also* machine twist

warp: the set of yarn in all woven fabrics that runs lengthwise and parallel to the selvage, and is interwoven with the filling.

washfastness: the resistance of a dyed fabric to loss of color or change in properties during home or commercial laundering.

weave: a system or pattern of intersecting warp and filling yarns. There are three basic weaves: plain, satin, and twill (not used extensively for quilt-making). All other weaves are derived from one or more of these types.

winding: the process of transferring yarn or thread from one type of package to another to facilitate subsequent processing.

yarn: a continuous strand of textile fibers or filaments suitable for knitting, weaving, or otherwise intertwining to form a textile fabric. Yarn is the basic material which is made into fabric, thread, or cords.

BIBLIOGRAPHY

American Association of Textile Chemists and Colorists. *AATCC Technical Manual*, Volume 66, 1991.

Barnhardt Manufacturing Co. Processing Bleached Cotton, A Technical Guide for the Nonwovens Producer.

Celanese Corporation. *Man-Made Fiber and Textile Dictionary.* Fourth Edition. 1981.

Cohen, Allen C. *Beyond Basic Textiles.* New York: Fairchild Publications. 1982.

Cotton Incorporated. *Cottons for Nonwovens: A Technical Guide.*

Finch, Karen and Greta Putnam. *The Care and Preservation of Textiles.* London: B.T. Batsford LTD. 1985.

Finley, Ruth E. *Old Patchwork Quilts and the Women Who Made Them.* Charles T. Branford Company. 1957

Goutman, Marylyn. *Survey of the Textile Industry, Laboratory Manual.* Philadelphia: College of Textiles and Science Philadelphia. 1988.

Hollen, Norma and Jane Saddler. *Textiles.* Third Edition. New York: Macmillan. 1970.

Joseph, Marjory L. *Essentials of Textiles.* Fourth Edition. New York: Holt, Rinehart, and Winston. 1988.

Joseph, Marjory L. *Introductory Textile Science.* Fifth Edition. New York: Holt, Rinehart and Winston. 1986.

Pizzuto, Joseph J. *Fabric Science.* Fifth Edition. New York: Fairchild. 1986.

Storey, Joyce. *The Thames and Hudson Manual of Dyes and Fabrics.* London: Thames and Hudson Ltd. 1978.

Turbak, Albin F. (editor). *Nonwovens: Theory, Process, Performance, and Testing.* Atlanta: Tappi Press. 1993.

Wagner, J. Robert. *Nonwoven Fabrics.* Norristown, PA: Self Published. 1982.

OTHER BOOKS FROM C&T PUBLISHING:

An Amish Adventure - 2nd Edition, Roberta Horton
Anatomy of a Doll, The Fabric Sculptor's Handbook, Susanna Oroyan
Appliqué 12 Easy Ways! Elly Sienkiewicz
Art & Inspirations: Ruth B. McDowell, Ruth B. McDowell
The Art of Silk Ribbon Embroidery, Judith Baker Montano
The Artful Ribbon, Beauties in Bloom, Candace Kling
Basic Seminole Patchwork, Cheryl Greider Bradkin
Colors Changing Hue, Yvonne Porcella
Crazy with Cotton, Piecing Together Memories & Themes, Diana Leone
Enduring Grace, Quilts from the Shelburne Museum Collection, Celia Y. Oliver
Faces & Places, Images in Appliqué, Charlotte Warr Andersen
Fractured Landscape Quilts, Katie Pasquini Masopust
From Fiber to Fabric, The Essential Guide to Quiltmaking Textiles, Harriet Hargrave
Heirloom Machine Quilting, Harriet Hargrave
Impressionist Quilts, Gai Perry
Kaleidoscopes & Quilts, Paula Nadelstern
Mariner's Compass Quilts, New Directions, Judy Mathieson
Mastering Machine Appliqué, Harriet Hargrave
The New Sampler Quilt, Diana Leone
Patchwork Persuasion, Fascinating Quilts From Traditional Designs, Joen Wolfrom
Patchwork Quilts Made Easy, Jean Wells (co-published with Rodale Press, Inc.)
Pieces of an American Quilt, Patty McCormick
Quilts, Quilts, and More Quilts! Diana McClun and Laura Nownes
Say It With Quilts, Diana McClun and Laura Nownes
Simply Stars, Quilts that Sparkle, Alex Anderson
Small Scale Quiltmaking, Precision, Proportion, and Detail, Sally Collins
Soft-Edge Piecing, Jinny Beyer
Start Quilting with Alex Anderson, Six Projects for First-time Quilters
Tradition with a Twist, Variations on Your Favorite Quilts, Blanche Young and Dalene Young Stone
Trapunto by Machine, Hari Walner
Visions: QuiltArt, Quilt San Diego
The Visual Dance, Creating Spectacular Quilts, Joen Wolfrom
Willowood, Further Adventures in Buttonhole Stitch Appliqué, Jean Wells
88 Leaders of the Quilt World, Nihon Vogue

For more information write for a free catalog from:
C&T Publishing
P.O. Box 1456
Lafayette, CA 94549
(1-800-284-1114)

For quilting supplies:
Cotton Patch Mail Order
3405 Hall Lane, Dept. CTB
Lafayette, CA 94549
e-mail: cottonpa@aol.com
800/835-4418
510/283-7883